Few plays have generated more controversy or had a more extraordinary performance history than Molière's *Don Juan.* David Whitton's study examines ways in which this enigmatic masterpiece has been interpreted in performance through the vision of different directors and in a variety of cultural and social contexts ranging from pre-revolutionary St Petersburg to post-revolutionary Prague. In a series of critical studies, key productions are re-constructed using prompt books, production notes, photographs, contemporary reviews, memoirs and the author's own experience as a spectator. Among the interpretations discussed are those of Meyerhold and Brecht, Bergman, Jouvet and Chéreau. Each of these productions, in addition to shedding new light on a familiar text, is a theatrical landmark in its own right.

The book is illustrated with numerous photographs and contains a geographical–chronological table of productions.

MOLIÈRE

DON JUAN

PLAYS IN PRODUCTION

Series editor: Michael Robinson

PUBLISHED VOLUMES

Ibsen: *A Doll's House* by Egil Törnqvist
Miller: *Death of a Salesman* by Brenda Murphy
Molière: *Don Juan* by David Whitton

MOLIÈRE

DON JUAN

DAVID WHITTON
Lancaster University

Published by the Press Syndicate of the University of Cambridge
The Pitt Building, Trumpington Street, Cambridge CB2 1RP
40 West 20th Street, New York, NY 10011–4211, USA
10 Stamford Road, Oakleigh, Melbourne 3166, Australia

First published 1995

Printed in Great Britain at the University Press, Cambridge

A Catalogue record for this book is available from the British Library

Library of Congress cataloguing in publication data

Whitton, David.
Molière, Don Juan / David Whitton.
p. cm.
Includes bibliographical references and indexes.
ISBN 0 521 43296 0 (hardback). – ISBN 0 521 47867 7 (paperback.)
1. Molière, 1622–1673. Don Juan. 2. Molière, 1622–1673 – Stage history. 3. Don Juan (legendary character) in literature.
I. Title.
PQ1831.W48 1995
842′.4 – dc20 94–14924 CIP

ISBN 0 521 43296 0 hardback
ISBN 0 521 47867 7 paperback

TAG

CONTENTS

PLATES

Photographic credits

1, 2, 7, 8, 9: Viollet-Lipnitzki; 3, 4, 6, 10, 19: Agence Bernand; 11, 12: St Petersburg Theatre Library (photos K. Fisher); 5, 20: Bricage; 15: Drottningholms Teatermuseum (photo Beata Bergström); 16: Salzburger Festspiel; 13, 14: Archiv Bertolt-Brecht; 17, 18: Viktor Kronbauer.

GENERAL PREFACE

Volumes in the series Plays in Production will take major dramatic texts and examine their transposition, firstly onto the stage and, secondly, where appropriate, into other media. Each book will include concise but informed studies of individual dramatic texts, focusing on the original theatrical and historical context of a play in relation to its initial performance and reception followed by subsequent major interpretations on stage, both under the impact of changing social, political and cultural values, and in response to developments in the theatre generally.

Many of the plays will also have been transposed into other media – film, opera, television, ballet – which may well be the form in which they are first encountered by a contemporary audience. Thus, a substantial study of the play text and the issues it raises for theatrical realisation will be supplemented by an assessment of such adaptations as well as the production history, where the emphasis will be on the development of a performance tradition for each work, including staging and acting styles, rather than simply the archaeological reconstruction of past performances.

Plays included in the series are all likely to receive regular performance and individual volumes will be of interest to the informed reader as well as to students of theatre history and literature. Each book also contains an annotated production chronology as well as numerous photographs from key performances.

Michael Robinson
University of East Anglia

PREFACE

Few plays can have generated more controversy or had a more extraordinary performance history than Molière's *Don Juan*. After a sensational première in 1665 the play ran into religious opposition almost immediately and was withdrawn – or banned? – after fifteen performances, never to be performed again in the author's lifetime. For the next one hundred and seventy-six years it was known in France only in Thomas Corneille's bowdlerised verse adaptation. Sporadic revivals during the late nineteenth and early twentieth centuries did little to correct the play's reputation as an aberrant, if not downright unplayable, text. In fact, it was not until Louis Jouvet's masterly production in 1947 that *Don Juan* was elevated to its rightful place as a central work of the classical repertoire. In recent decades there has hardly been a single French director of note who has not offered his or her *Don Juan*. Elsewhere in Europe, meanwhile, it has inspired theatre practitioners as diverse as Meyerhold, Besson, Bergman and Grossman to some of their greatest directorial achievements.

All these directors have brought their own vision and methods to bear on a text which is acknowledged to be one of the most unorthodox and ambiguous works of the repertoire. The result of their experiments has been to reveal the play in a startling variety of guises, from the comic to the tragic, and in a range of perspectives from Christian to atheist and from absurdist to Marxist. The one thing they have all shared is a belief in its actuality, a conviction that Molière's three-centuries-old play had something relevant to say to the audiences of their time. My purpose in this study, therefore, is to examine ways in which Molière's text has been mediated in performance through the vision of different practitioners, and to enquire what those performances might have meant to their spectators. Key productions have been reconstructed using the familiar source materials of theatre historiography: prompt books and production notes, photographs, contemporary reviews, memoirs, reminiscences and, for a number of more recent productions, my own experiences as spectator. The book consists mostly of a series of individual production studies. Collectively, they recount the theatrical life of a play which has enjoyed a remarkable stage presence.

The production history of a single play is also, in a sense, a history of theatre itself and indirectly of the society in which theatre arises. The successive faces assumed by a major work of the repertoire reflect the changing theatrical priorities and broader cultural preoccupations of the time. With this in mind, I have aimed to offer a selection of productions which represent important phases in the development of the modern stage from modernism to postmodernism. The Don Juan legend is a global phenomenon, and it would undoubtedly have been interesting to trace its wider reverberations in the theatre of, say, Africa or America. But to extend the coverage to other continents and other languages would have weakened the contextual focus. For that reason I have chosen to restrict my study to major European theatres. Within those parameters, the choices were largely self-selecting. Each of the productions discussed here, as well as shedding new light on a familiar text, is a theatrical landmark in its own right.

ACKNOWLEDGEMENTS

I would like to thank some of the many people who supported or assisted with this work.

The British Academy, for enabling me to carry out the research with a personal research grant.

The artistic and administrative staff at the Bayerisches Staatsschauspiel, Comédie de Genève, Deutsches Theater, Na zábradlí Theatre, Royal Exchange Theatre Company, Maison des Arts de Créteil, Théâtre Municipal de Gennevilliers, Théâtre National de Chaillot.

The staff of the following archives and libraries: Bibliothèque de l'Arsenal, Bibliothèque Gaston Baty and Bibliothèque de la Comédie-Française (Paris); Bertolt-Brecht-Archiv, Institut für Theaterwissenschaft, Freie Universität (Berlin); Theatermuseum, Universität zu Köln (Cologne); Central State Archive for Literature and Art (Moscow); St Petersburg Theatre Museum (St Petersburg); Drottningholms Teatermuseum (Stockholm); Theatre Institute (Prague).

The editors of *Nottingham French Studies* and *Le Nouveau Molièriste* for permission to re-use material from my articles on Jan Grossman and the Comédie-Française.

Irina Peller, Jane Kasam, Katerina Ferenčikova, Francis Turton, Dorothee Williamson, for help with translations; and, in particular, Lindsay Newman, librarian *extraordinaire*, of Lancaster University.

My wife and children, for their forbearance.

CHAPTER 1

'DON JUAN', 1665–1925

MOLIÈRE AND THE LEGEND OF DON JUAN

Tales about statues of the dead coming to life to exact retribution from the living were endemic in medieval folk legend, and in literature stretching back to antiquity. But the fusion of the Stone Guest motif with the story of an unrepentant womaniser first appeared in Spain in 1630. Written by a monk, Tirso de Molina, *The Joker of Seville and the Guest of Stone* recounts the life of Don Juan Tenorio, whose adventures are punished when the statue of a Commander whom he had killed, and whose daughter he has tried to seduce, invites him to supper and drags him down to Hell. This cautionary tale, despite its pious intentions, is actually a much more exciting play than it sounds, as a recent production by the Royal Shakespeare Company proved.[1] In addition to its sensational story, the play broaches two major themes which, at the emergence of the modern world, were starting to take a grip on Western consciousness: the clash between the rationalist mind and phenomena which transcend the material world, and the tension between the individual ego and the moral restraints of society. Unwittingly, Tirso had created a mythical archetype which has inspired innumerable poets, playwrights, novelists and composers.

From Spain, the story quickly passed to Italy, and from there to France. Giliberto's *The Guest of Stone* (1652) is now lost, but another play of the same name, attributed to Cicognini, inspired versions by the French playwrights Dorimon (1658) and Villiers (1659). During the course of its transmission, the story acquired an increasingly comic or tragi-comic complexion. In the process, the figure of the servant Catalinón assumed growing importance as a counterweight to Don Juan. The story was becoming that of a couple, with the servant (Molière's Sganarelle, Mozart's Leporello) having equal dramatic status to the master. In addition, the focus was shifting from the moral lesson to the central character's motivation, thus laying the groundwork for the emergence of *Don Juan* as a modern psychological type rather than Tirso's morality-play Everyman. The story, meanwhile, had also been absorbed into the repertoire of *commedia dell'arte* where it became a subject of farce, and this gave it a second line of transmission to France. One scenario by Biancolelli, a popular Harlequin, was being performed in Paris in the early 1660s. At about the same time the Italian Players, with whom Molière was then sharing the Petit-Bourbon theatre, were performing their own version.

What attracted Molière to the story was doubtless its proven box-office appeal. The latter was always a crucial consideration to the playwright and actor-manager, but especially so in 1664-5 when he wrote *Don Juan*. For three years he had been fighting off attacks from the coalition of churchmen, prudes and theatrical rivals whose enmity had been aroused by the phenomenenal success in 1662 of *School for Wives*. In May 1664 he suffered a serious blow at the hands of the Company of Jesus with the suppression of *Tartuffe* after only a single performance at Versailles. The need for a new play to revive the repertoire must have been very pressing. But the loss of *Tartuffe* was clearly more than a financial set-back. The tenacity with which he waged his five-year struggle to get the ban lifted suggests that for Molière it was, above all, a moral issue. What was at stake was his survival as an artist who asserted the right of comedy to be serious, that is to treat the burning social and philosophical issues of his time. In this perspective the full extent of Molière's boldness in writing *Don Juan* becomes apparent. Faced with calls from the highest religious authorities for his elimination, he chose to riposte not with a safe and innocuous comedy but with a work which was, if anything, more audacious than *Tartuffe*.

Molière's *Don Juan* is not a simple re-telling of the story but an original play adapted to the manners and ideas of his time. Ostensibly the action is set in Sicily but contemporaries would easily recognise in Don Juan the portrait of an emancipated French nobleman of the mid-seventeenth century. Depicting a gallery of contemporary social types, the play functions at one level as a comedy of manners. At another level, in keeping with the classical interest in human nature, it becomes a portrait of an individual. Molière transfers the interest from the Don's sexual exploits, which are reduced to illustrative incidents, to his psychology. He endows him with a powerful intellect and allows him to justify his actions in terms of a systematic programme of rational free-thinking. Don Juan, unlike his real-life counterparts who dabbled in Epicurianism and materialistic scepticism, may simply be using his professed philosophy as a convenient cloak for a selfish way of life. But by treating the subject at the level of philosophical debate, Molière makes the play into a provocative blend of social satire and metaphysical speculation. Another major contribution to the legend was to make Sganarelle Don Juan's close confidant. More than a comic foil, his real dramatic function – which directors ignore at their peril – is to break through the master's monstrous inaccessibility and to reveal Don Juan to the audience.

We may take it for granted that a play should be judged on its own terms, by what it is rather than what it is not. But to understand why *Don Juan* was for so long consigned to neglect, one needs to recognise that in terms of the formal rules of French classical dramaturgy it is a highly unorthodox masterpiece. It is written in prose rather than verse; it defies the three unities of place, time and action; instead of a single plot there are three strands to the intrigue (the pursuit of Don Juan by his wronged wife Elvire and her three brothers; Don Juan's amorous pursuit of the peasant women; the unrelated episode of the Commander who returns from Don Juan's past to inflict retribution). The plot is episodic, with a sequence of sometimes unrelated characters and scenes, the exposition is incomplete, and some actions are initiated inconclusively. Disconcertingly, Molière also confounds the classical convention by mixing dramatic genres: neither comedy nor tragedy, the play is a tragi-comedy in which broad farce is juxtaposed with semi-serious discussion of weighty moral and philosophical issues. It is these non-classical qualities (sometimes described as 'Shakespearean'), that condemned *Don Juan* to its status in the eighteenth and nineteenth centuries as a chaotically incoherent work – and, conversely, have helped to make its appeal irresistible to modern directors and audiences.

Critics have often felt compelled to explain the play's irregularities in terms of the supposed haste with which it was written. In fact, recent evidence shows that Molière composed it over a rather longer period than was formerly imagined. In any case, rather than seeking explanations for allegedly defective craftsmanship, it seems more profitable to enquire what artistic principles govern its composition.

Beneath an apparently erratic action there lies, in fact, a deep structural unity. Briefly, the action is constructed around a pivotal point between the third and fourth acts. The first three acts depict Don Juan in a series of adventures, eluding Elvire and her brothers while all the time pursuing whatever objects of interest present themselves to him (a passing flirtation with peasant women, an entanglement with brigands, a moral duel with a hermit). All these episodes are introduced as illustrations of the libertine's way of life, the reasons for which are illuminated, meanwhile, in a series of philosophical discussions with Sganarelle. The fact that each act, contrary to classical convention, has a different setting, is intrinsic to the play's meaning, as too is the fact that each location is out of doors. At a symbolic level, the discontinuity of the action and the topographical variety express Don Juan's relationship with the world. The spectator watches the libertine roaming freely, irresponsibly and with seeming impunity, through the world of others. At the very end of the third act the play takes a leap into the supernatural with the first appearance of the Commander, suggesting that there may be more to the world than Don Juan's materialistic philosophy allows. The last two acts, in contrast to the first three, show the net closing in and for that reason are markedly less episodic. The fourth act switches to an interior setting – a significant change since the central character is no longer seen as an unhindered free spirit. A now immobile Don Juan is being visited by a succession of creditors, literal and metaphorical, each of whom delivers a request, which is denied, and a warning, which is tossed aside. They present themselves in a sequence that reflects the increasing gravity of their mission: the tradesman (money), the father (family honour), the wife (Christian duty), the Commander (perdition). Don Juan's refusal to heed their demands invokes a process of retribution, which the final act executes. First, as in all classical tragedies and comedies, there is a scene where the onward rush of events is suspended: in one final escapade Don Juan, assuming the mask of a religious hypocrite, enjoys what the spectators now sense is only an illusion of impunity; from then on, the action accelerates towards its ordained conclusion. Described thus, the play is anything but chaotic. Certainly, directors who have approached it on its own terms have found in it a perfectly coherent, implacable, artistic logic.

What these actions signify in ethical and social terms is, however, altogether more problematic. Of all Molière's plays, *Don Juan* poses the greatest interpretative difficulties. This is partly because the central character himself appears to be a paradoxical mixture of positive and negative qualities. If the abusive treatment of his servant, wife, father and chance acquaintances is reprehensible, there is something admirable, to the modern mind, in his intellectual emancipation and defiance of authority. Is he a progressive thinker ripping off the mask of conventional morality or a ruthless, unscrupulous egoist? When, confronted with the miraculous apparition that will kill him, he refutes the evidence of his eyes and reaffirms his rationalist beliefs, should this be seen as intellectual courage or foolish obduracy? The comedy in the play offers few pointers to how we should evaluate him – indeed, it compounds the ambiguity of Don Juan as a character. In satire, laughter generally serves to direct criticism.

In *Don Juan*, however, we invariably laugh *with* Don Juan at his victims, producing an unusual and unsettling antithesis between the play's comic structure and its moral structure. While condemning his conduct, we are invited to admire the effortless superiority with which he despatches his opponents' arguments.

Since Don Juan is a professed atheist, the absence of any character who can effectively oppose him is no trivial matter. Molière uses the intimate master-servant relationship as the platform for a religious debate. But the way the debate is conducted is heavily loaded, with only a credulous and superstitious valet to oppose the master's superior intelligence. Ostensibly, the debate is ultimately resolved by a higher agent. The ending, in which the Statue takes Don Juan to Hell, appears finally to give the lie to his rationalism and to satisfy the moralists' desire to see the sinner punished. In practice it does nothing of the sort, as Molière's enemies instantly realised. The recourse to an arbitrary *deus ex machina* robs the ending of its plausibility and the play of any clear moral lesson. Sganarelle's final comments pay lip service to conventional morality:

> Now he's dead and everyone's satisfied – the Heaven he offended, the laws he broke, the families he disgraced, the parents he outraged, the wives he perverted, the husbands he destroyed.

But even these platitudes are devalued by the bathetic final cry: 'My wages, what about my wages?'

For the playwright, Don Juan may have been less enigmatic than he appears to us. Molière is known to have associated with genuine free-thinkers, and it is more than possible that he sympathised with their progressive attitudes. But to conclude from this that he sympathised with Don Juan, or intended him as his spokesman in the expression of rationalist ideas, seems very dubious. The most likely explanation (though this can only be a matter for speculation) is that he wished to show an aristocratic egoist who adopts the arguments of a free-thinker to justify his socially irresponsible behaviour. If we strip the play of its obfuscating religious debate, the central idea as

Molière conceived it may be the demonstration of Sganarelle's famous statement in the opening scene that 'a wicked nobleman is a terrible thing'. The increasingly heroic perceptions of Don Juan as an enlightened thinker, a scourge of petty-minded moralists, or as a God-defying figure like Faust, would then reflect the preoccupations of later generations less involved in the social reality that Molière was dealing with.

This is not in the least to suggest that other interpretations are 'wrong'. Works of the past only live in the present insofar as they are constantly re-interpreted in terms which are relevant to the spectators' own experience. And whatever Molière really felt about Don Juan, he created a disconcertingly ambivalent figure. The action raises questions to which the dénouement supplies a formal solution but no satisfactory answers, because none is realistically possible. Ultimately, what guarantees the play its enduring fascination is precisely that it is not a demonstration of a moral theorem but an exploration of problems to which no simple solutions are forthcoming.

THE PLAY'S PREMIÈRE

One practical consequence of Molière's desire to capitalise on the theatrical vogue of *Don Juan* was the requirement for a more elaborate form of staging than the single stage setting in which most of his comedies, written to conform to the classical unity of place, were performed. *Don Juan* belongs to a different contemporary genre, that of the machine-play. Spectacular stage effects were a feature of productions at the rival Marais theatre and of the court entertainments to which Molière contributed, but they were a new departure for the playwright's Palais-Royal theatre – so new, in fact, that he took the unusual step of commissioning special sets from stage decorators. In the absence of any surviving visual evidence, it is the recently discovered contract for the sets that provides the best information we have about how the play was staged.

Molière ordered a series of six *trompe-l'œil* perspective sets, one for each of the five acts, plus a transformation effect during the third act. The first act required: 'a palace comprising five wings on each side and a façade at the rear, the first wings being eighteen *pieds* high and the others diminishing in perspective'. To give added depth to the picture, the backcloth had a cut-out which opened on to 'two smaller wings depicting a garden, and a distant perspective'. In the second act, the architectural perspective was replaced by a country scene consisting of five pairs of wings with a backdrop representing a grotto and, again, a cut-out, this time framing a seascape. The third act, where the supernatural makes its first appearance, was fittingly the most spectacular. It began with a shallow stage – three pairs of wings representing a forest – and was enclosed at the rear with a wall painted to represent a temple. Towards the end of the act Don Juan notices the temple and, on being told by Sganarelle that it is the Commander's tomb, decides to enter it. Here the text contains the stage direction: 'the tomb opens to reveal a superb mausoleum and the Commander's statue'. This implies that the back wall was drawn apart to reveal a further scene beyond. In reality, something more elaborate than a revelation scene must have occurred, because the fifth setting was: 'the interior of a temple, comprising five sets of wings, the first eighteen *pieds* high and the others diminishing in perspective, and a closed wall representing the back of the temple'. As this makes clear, there was a full transformation effect, with one complete setting being replaced by an entirely new one. While the upstage wall was drawn apart to reveal the deepest interior of the tomb, the forest simultaneously disappeared into the wings to be replaced by the monumental marble of the tomb, whilst new overhead borders (also specified in the contract) were flown in to replace the sky borders of the previous scene. After a more modest, fully enclosed interior representing Don Juan's apartment in the fourth act, the fifth-act setting gave a grand finale: 'a town, comprising five wings on each side ... and at the back a painted town gate, with two smaller wings and a perspective beyond'. From these specifications together with the costume inventory it is clear that great attention (and considerable expense – nine hundred *livres* for the sets) was devoted to making the production visually very impressive.

In this connection, a curious feature of the play is the way the dialogue refers, quite insistently, to the settings in which the characters find themselves. In the first act Sganarelle indicates his master to Gusman with the words: 'Look, there he is, *walking in this palace*.' In the second act Don Juan greets Charlotte by saying: 'Good heavens! Are there really delicious creatures like you to be found in this countryside, *amongst these trees and rocks*?' From a utilitarian point of view the specific details are superfluous, serving only to draw attention to something that the spectators can already see for themselves. Again, in Act III, when Don Juan and Sganarelle enter the temple, the latter exclaims: 'Oh, isn't it beautiful! The statues! Oh, the beautiful marble, and those pillars!' These repeated references to location clearly must have interacted with the staging to affect the audience's experience of the play, and have led some critics to speak of a deliberate Brechtian alienation effect. This seems to me, however, to be a misunderstanding of baroque illusion, which never aspired to be a 'real' deception; the pleasure came rather from the spectator's knowing complicity in the illusion. Rather than trying to 'break' an illusion which was only ever a deception of the senses, not of the understanding, Molière was offering a comic version of it. Coming from the mouth of the credulous Sganarelle – the only person in the theatre apparently taken in by the illusion – the admiring comments on painted stage props can only have provoked laughter. Molière seems, in fact, to have succeeded in having it both ways: showing that he could produce stage effects to rival those of the Marais company, whilst enhancing the spectators' enjoyment of them by nudging references to their staginess. This is not to say that the humour is entirely innocent. Its subversive potential becomes clear with Sganarelle's demonstration of God's existence by the design argument. 'I should like to know', he asks, 'who made those trees, those rocks, this ground we are standing on, and that sky up there. Did it all create itself?' Sganarelle's gestures to painted cardboard and canvas made an obvious mockery of his proof of divine purpose.

The role of Don Juan was played by La Grange, the most dependable and faithful of Molière's actors. The costume he wore is described for us by Sganarelle. With a tightly-curled blond wig, feathered hat, gold threads in his coat and flame-coloured ribbons, he was the last word in elegance and high fashion. No contemporary account of his performance as *Don Juan* has been found, but his qualities as an actor are well known: he was 'good-looking, with an easy manner, natural and relaxed' (Chappuzeau). With such urbane and attractive qualities, he was the ideal interpreter of his habitual role in Molière's comedies: that of the sincere young lover. In entrusting the part to La Grange, Molière was clearly not intent on blackening his hero. He may have been blasé, with the cynicism not uncommon among sophisticated courtiers of the period, but it is impossible to imagine that his Don Juan had any of the mythic dimensions, whether satanic or Promethean, that the role acquired in later centuries. All the evidence points to a more realistic portrayal of a social type – the irresponsible nobleman – whose youth (La Grange was twenty-six at the time) and affable manner must have attenuated the darker side of his conduct. It is certainly notable that even the play's most vociferous critics recorded little in the way of objections to Don Juan. It was Sganarelle that they found scandalous.

Sganarelle, of course, was Molière's role. Although it goes far beyond simple farce, the role is constructed on the lines of a character from farce at which Molière, with his vigorous and highly coloured acting style, was unsurpassable. It can safely be assumed that the many *lazzi* and farce routines that he wrote into the part were played to the hilt, though his costume of cast-offs from his master's wardrobe (gold satin jupon, cotton camisole with gold decorations, and satin doublet with flower motifs) suggests that something more realistic than the conventional valet of farce was aimed at. Again, there is no direct evidence of how Molière performed the role, but an idea of it can be inferred from the impression it produced on contemporaries. Rochemont's polemical blast was directed mainly against the 'valet [who is] even more impious than the master'. Molière, he said, depicts 'a fool who makes grotesque speeches about God and undermines his arguments with a deliberate pratfall'.[2] For the Prince de Conti, similarly, the real scandal was not the atheist master but that the fact that the playwright 'entrusts God's cause to a valet and, in order to defend Him, makes him say all sorts of inanities'.[3] Conti especially criticised the way Molière, by his comic acting in the final scene, ridiculed the edifying lesson of Don Juan's horrible end. Rochemont adds the intriguing detail that 'the thunder makes the valet laugh'.

The production opened on 15 February 1665. Audience figures and box-office receipts were high (the takings for the fifth performance were amongst the highest recorded in the period) and remained solid for the duration of the first run. But the play immediately ran into opposition from the Cabal. 'All Paris is talking about Molière's crime' began one anonymous sonnet that was circulated in the salons. To save his play Molière offered concessions: by the second performance (17 February) a number of controversial lines had been cut, and the scene where Don Juan tempts a Beggar with money on condition that he blasphemes was removed in its entirety. Evidently these changes did not satisfy the Cabal, since the polemic continued to rage for some months. But the exact reasons for what happened next remain a matter for conjecture. What is known is that on 20 March the theatres closed for Lent and when they reopened Don Juan had been withdrawn from the repertoire.

No one has succeeded in explaining its abrupt disappearance. It is commonly thought to have been withdrawn as a result of pressure brought to bear on Molière by the devout set close to the King, though no documentary evidence survives to prove the theory. Nor, in fact, is there anything to suggest that the pleasure-loving Louis XIV disapproved of the play personally. On the contrary, four months later he officially extended his patronage and protection to

Molière's company, which took the title of King's Players (*Troupe du Roi au Palais-Royal*). Perhaps, then, it had been intimated to Molière that a reward would be forthcoming if he exercised discretion over *Don Juan*. Alternatively, it may be that Molière's priority was to rescue *Tartuffe*, which was still banned, and that he chose to sacrifice *Don Juan* in the interests of winning the long-term battle over *Tartuffe*. But one can be sure that Molière would not have taken a lucrative play off the bill without good reason. Clearly, whatever the mechanism involved, the opposition had somehow forced the play's withdrawal. Even then, their anger was not placated. The controversy raged on over the following months, during which Molière was accused of mounting a deliberate attack on organised religion by exposing piety to ridicule and defying heaven's vengeance by means of 'ridiculous fireworks'. The ferocity of these pamphlets offers a telling record of the anti-theatrical climate into which Molière ventured to pitch his play.

'DON JUAN' ON STAGE, 1665–1925

Molière never performed *Don Juan* again, nor was it published during his lifetime.[4] In 1677, four years after his death, his widow Madeleine Béjart commissioned from Thomas Corneille an adaptation which became a popular play. Corneille 'improved' the play from a literary point of view by versifying it, and introduced a number of new characters. In something of an understatement he also said he had 'softened certain passages which had offended sensitive people'. The Beggar scene was eliminated, the discussion of Don Juan's beliefs likewise, and the re-written ending became a straightforward warning to others. The new play ended with Sganarelle saying: 'The earth has swallowed him up! I will hasten to become a hermit. All scoundrels will be filled with dismay by this warning example. Woe to him who sees it and does not profit from it.' In this emasculated form *Don Juan* was rendered acceptable. It was played twenty-six times by Molière's company, and more than five hundred times by the Comédie-Française (created in 1680 by a merger of the playwright's company with the Hôtel de Bourgogne) during the next century and a half. But it was not Molière's play.

Throughout the eighteenth century, which saw the appearance of another Don Juan masterpiece in Da Ponte's and Mozart's *Don Giovanni*, *Don Juan* was considered unworthy of inclusion in the canon of Molière's great comedies. The later Romantic period saw the start of a critical revaluation with writers like Musset and Gautier showing renewed interest in the work. Their interest was literary rather than theatrical and their reading, inevitably, was coloured by Romantic manifestions of Don Juan, especially those of Hoffmann (which had an enormous impact in France following its publication in French in 1829) and Byron. In 1841, however, Robert Kemp, the young actor-director of the Odéon theatre, conceived the notion of producing Molière's original *Don Juan*. The idea was a bold one which challenged both the low esteem in which the play was held and the Comédie-Française's presumed monopoly on Molière. There were ten performances, with Kemp in the title role. Since the highlight of the production was the appearance of the actor Barré in the minor role of Pierrot, they can have contributed little to a revised understanding of the play. Seven years later, however, spurred on by Kemp's initiative, the Comédie-Française mounted its first production of Molière's *Don Juan* (15 January 1847).

The first appearance of any play in the Comédie-Française's repertoire is always vested with symbolic importance. The restoration of *Don Juan*, timed to celebrate the two hundred and twenty-fifth anniversary of the playwright's birth, was no exception. A contemporary gazette heralded 'a *Don Juan* freed from suppressions and modifications', promised 'a spectacular dénouement in conformity with the author's intentions', and advised its readers that 'boxes and stalls are being booked as if they are being given away free'.[5]

It was, indeed, a lavish production with magnificent period costumes created by Achille Devéria and five settings painted by the celebrated stage decorator Ciceri. The contemporary tendency towards scenic realism is evident in both sets and costumes, giving an effect which is impressive but somewhat heavy and (by today's values) lacking in poetry. Rather unusually, the first-act setting was the interior of a palace, fully furnished in Louis XIV style, and with double windows opening on to a terrace and garden. The fourth act, showing a furnished apartment resplendent in red and gold, was similarly replete with naturalistic detail down to a fully-laid table of plates, glasses, and cutlery. Ciceri was a master of stage machinery, and the special effects of Statue, spectral figures, trapdoors, flames and smoke, were produced with particular brilliance. No contradiction was apparently perceived between the realism of the scenery and the miraculous effects.

In the two principal roles neither performer was entirely happy. Geffroy, the actor playing Don Juan, was celebrated for his success in Romantic dramas but on this occasion his 'sombre, fateful physiognomy' (Hugo) was badly suited to the role. His performance did not correspond to the public's preconceived image of a Casanova-like seducer and, not suprisingly, was thought to lack charm and wit. As for the servant, he was interpreted by Samson who had been playing Sganarelle in the Thomas Corneille version since the 1820s. In a period when declamatory performance was commonplace, he was famous for his measured, understated acting. Inevitably, this resulted in a Sganarelle who offered insufficient contrast to Don Juan and made little impact in itself – indeed, the role was virtually eclipsed in this production. Plaudits went instead to Régnier's infinitely more animated Pierrot, to Mme Volnys, whose Elvire was praised for her natural, gracious manner, and above all to the grand veteran Ligier whose moving performance as the Beggar was judged the high point of the production!

There were further sporadic revivals between 1847 and 1876. Rather than being new productions, these re-used the set and prompt book of Régnier's 1847 staging, as was the practice at the time. Unquestionably the most striking Don Juan of this period was Bressant who replaced Geffroy in 1858. Bressant was as charming and seductive as Geffroy was brooding and ungracious. According to a contemporary, he was 'the most elegant Don Juan one can imagine. His costumes are delicious; he wears them exquisitely; he comes and goes with perfect ease.'[6] It was a brilliant but one-dimensional portrait of a consummate seducer.

After these tentative revivals in the middle decades of the century, none of which succeeded in wresting Molière from the Romantic tradition, the play returned once more to obscurity. Forty years elapsed before the Comédie-Française's next unhappy attempt to revive it (15 January 1917). The role of Don Juan fell to the veteran actor Rafaël Duflos who also directed the production. Duflos wrote that he considered the part one of the heaviest and least rewarding in the repertoire and made no secret of the fact that he accepted it only out of a sense of duty[7] – and it showed. He gave the impression of an aged, tired actor impersonating an aged, tired Don Juan. Critics were unanimous in their condemnation: 'M. Duflos wears his beautiful costumes with style, but it's not enough... From start to finish he is bored, and he bores us.'[8] Georges Berr, a popular actor of the old school, played Sganarelle as a stereotypical comic servant. As with Duflos, there was no exploration of the role: 'M. Berr seems to imagine that this incarnation of the people is merely a repertoire valet like any other. And he plays the part with all his stock-in-trade mannerisms. It is an odious spectacle.'[9]

The production had a more favourable reception when it was revived in 1922 (and again, for Molière's tricentenary celebration, in 1925) with Maurice Escande replacing Duflos as Don Juan. Escande rejuvenated the role without suggesting any hidden depths beneath the seducer's charming exterior. But cast changes could not disguise the void of interpretation in what were, at bottom, perfunctory gestures which the Comédie-Française felt obliged to make periodically. The real problem was lack of belief in the play. Eighty years of half-hearted experiment had done little to overturn the received opinion that *Don Juan* was a hastily-written, flawed text which could not be made to work on the stage. Nor was there any sense that it might have anything relevant to say to modern audiences. The game was given away by a critic who wrote in 1917: 'Performances of Molière's *Don Juan* are mounted out of love of literature rather than for theatrical pleasure. It may not be a *bad* play, but it's an unfinished work and unsatisfying in performance.'[10]

There was, however, one man of the theatre who was convinced that *Don Juan* had more to offer than the current lazy, convention-bound productions of the time suggested. Jacques Copeau, whose productions of Molière at the Vieux-Colombier were as fresh and original as those of the Comédie-Française were stale and conventional, witnessed the anniversary performance in the Salle Richelieu on 15 January 1917. Recording his impressions in his Journal that night, he wrote indignantly about the pretentious, meaningless sets, the musical interludes, the overblown operatic staging and the vacuity of interpretation:

> In the second act, more music, then curtain up. Some little dancers perform a dance, sing, form a chain, disappear, whereupon, amidst an utterly pointless crowd of peasants, Charlotte and Pierrot appear and finally embark on their dialogue. And so it continues. The fourth act (the supper) involves another elaborate entertainment. People dressed in floating gauze mill around Don Juan, pour him drinks, brush roses against his head. In the middle of this Folies-Bergères show we have the Italian interlude of Sganarelle with the little lackey, acted timidly and without any warmth. The last act begins with a funereal chant and a cortege of hooded capucin monks... The whole thing is stupid and hideous.

Then Copeau gives a tantalising glimpse of his own vision of Molière:

> I am describing only what is redundant. It would take all day to talk about what is lacking. What is absent is simplicity and truth, everything that springs from a proper understanding of the text and an imaginative staging of it.[11]

He concludes: 'My mind is made up. I will include *Don Juan* in the Vieux-Colombier's next season.' Sadly, the production, which he had apparently been projecting since 1913, never materialised. Thus it fell to Copeau's pupil and successor Louis Jouvet, thirty years later, to reveal *Don Juan* to French audiences.

CHAPTER 2

MAJOR PRODUCTIONS ON THE MODERN FRENCH STAGE

A MYSTICAL TRAGEDY (LOUIS JOUVET, DIRECTOR)

Théâtre de l'Athénée, 24 December 1947

When it became known that the great actor-director Louis Jouvet was to stage *Don Juan*, the production was anticipated as the theatrical event of the period. For two decades, since taking over the mantle of Jacques Copeau when the latter closed his Vieux-Colombier theatre, Jouvet had been the dominant presence in French theatre and a key figure in the scenic revolution which transformed the French stage between the wars. His productions, all characterised by a polished theatricalism, were widely considered to represent a summit of artistry and stylistic perfection. Although contemporary French playwrights were the staple of his repertoire, one of his greatest successes in the 1930s had been a brilliant production of *School for Wives* which took a rather stale and neglected classic and transformed it into a sparkling stylised comedy. But there were many who doubted whether even Jouvet, for all his theatrical brilliance, could restore *Don Juan* in the way he had restored the five-act high comedy. Jouvet, too, saw it as one of the greatest challenges of his career.

His production was the culmination of years of reflection on the play which had convinced him that it was the forgotten masterpiece of seventeenth-century theatre. Jouvet was not one of those directors whose grasp of a text was intuitive; instead, he worked painstakingly, exploring a text, probing it and constantly revising his ideas. His aim in all this was to make the play yield up its secrets. He was suspicious of directors who try to impose themselves; in contrast to men like Craig, Meyerhold and Piscator, his ideal was rooted in the notion of fidelity to the text. Speaking of *Don Juan*, he said:

> Our production is not a demonstration of a theory or a polemical statement. Our sole guide is Molière... With *Don Juan* all one has to do is address the text. Everything else is superfluous... When you are approaching a masterpiece, the only possible attitude is a submissive one.[1]

This was the approach of a practitioner who, rather than trying to draw the play to himself, sought to put the techniques of his craft at the service of the play. In order to understand a play, he felt he had to discover its inner workings and mechanisms, its dramatic rhythms and the prosody of the speeches. He once remarked that taking a watch mechanism apart and putting it together again was child's play compared with finding out how a play works.

In the case of *Don Juan*, he had been studying the text on and off for more than thirty years. As early as 1908 he had acted the part of Don Louis in a soirée at the Groupe d'Action d'Art. His first serious thinking about the play seems to have begun during the First World War when he read a pious text by Saint François de Sales and was greatly struck by a similarity between the tenor of its expression and certain passages in the play.[2] *Don Juan* was also a text he worked on regularly with students at the Conservatoire in the 1930s. In Havana in 1943, during his war-time tour of Latin-America, he 'suffered a renewed attack of Don Juanitis', as a member of the company put it, and began to draft detailed staging notes.[3] Jouvet, who had previously been hesitating between Don Juan and Sganarelle, now decided to play Don Juan himself but was at a loss who to cast as his partner. Back in Paris in 1945 his eyes fell on a former music-hall comedian, Fernand-René, whose naive style of tender clowning exactly matched Jouvet's conception of the role. From that point, he was possessed by *Don Juan.* A long note which he dictated to his designer Christian Bérard in December 1945 reveals that by then – a full year before it went into rehearsal – all the key ideas about the staging and the dramatic effects he wanted to achieve were in place.[4] Rehearsals began in 1946. Michel Etcheverry, who stood in as Don Juan while Jouvet directed from the auditorium, tells how they would spend an afternoon working on a single line, and how days on end were spent perfecting movements in the scene where Don Juan flirts simultaneously with Charlotte and Mathurine.[5] Altogether nearly two hundred rehearsals were devoted to the production.

After four years of intensive preparation and a full year's rehearsal, the production opened at the Théâtre de l'Athénée on Christmas Eve 1947. It was a towering production, dominated by a massive performance from Jouvet as an aloof, solitary figure haunted by an obsession with a God whose existence he denies. As an interpretation of the play it was highly controversial but it enjoyed a huge public success, running for over two hundred performances – double the total for all the previous two centuries. Its impact in the longer term was enormous. By revealing the play's dramatic potential and uncovering new depths in the subject, it unlocked the play and opened a path for a flood of new interpretations that have made *Don Juan* one of the most popular works of the classical repertoire.

One of the challenges facing him, apart from the play's reputation, was the burden of the legend. In the public's mind *Don Juan* simply meant the adventures of a womaniser, and Jouvet knew that any production had to overcome the spectators' preconceived idea of the subject.[6] The specific nature of Molière's character had long been obscured by Da Ponte's debauchée and Byron's Romantic hero, but in addition there was now a more modern stereotype. Inspired partly by the spread of Freudianism and popularised by fiction and cinema – notably John Barrymore (1926) and Douglas Fairbanks (1934) – 'le donjuanisme' was a widespread motif in popular psychology and journalism between the wars. Errol Flynn's Don Juan, the ultimate Hollywood icon of the irresistible sexual force on whom even the most chaste and respectable daughters and wives could not help throwing themselves, was being filmed as Jouvet prepared his production of Molière.

Needless to say, Jouvet was not interested in any of that. As he observed (and he was the first director to notice this) seduction is a relatively insignificant element in Molière's play. Molière's Don Juan, he bluntly declared, is 'a seducer who seduces no-one'.[7] The theme of seduction features in only two scenes, and in both of these Jouvet distanced the character from his words and actions. The first was the famous speech to Sganarelle where Don Juan vaunts his delight in amorous conquest. Instead of arguing the speech Jouvet recited it rapidly and dismissively, showing that he did not take a word of it seriously. To critics who objected, he was able to reply that he was scrupulously following Molière's text, since Sganarelle's reaction is to declare: 'Bless me, how you can talk. It sounds like you know it by heart.' Again, the two-handed seduction of Charlotte and Mathurine was played in a rapid, disengaged style, and he gave the impression that his mind was elsewhere. This remote, aloof manner was disliked by some critics, but it fitted an interpretation of the play which turned the spotlight away from Don Juan's relations with other humans and on to the inner spiritual drama of his dealings with God. In fact, Jouvet gave a completely new face to the figure of Don Juan. The first night was his sixtieth birthday. The fact of envisaging Don Juan as a mature character rather than as a part for a young male lead signalled a rejection of the frivolous Casanova–Lovelace stereotype in favour of something infinitely more weighty. In effect, Jouvet was making Don Juan a responsible character, a man who is aware that he is confronting his ultimate destiny, rather than an irresponsible young rake. The result was to de-trivialise the subject and to inject a new gravity to the character's actions.

To say that Jouvet took the play's subject seriously is an understatement. In his personal notes (which may not have been intended for publication but are perhaps all the more revealing for that) he remarked that *Don Juan* was 'the only play which it really matters for every person to see once in their lifetime.'[8] This is an extravagant claim to make for any play, but Jouvet believed it was justified because he saw that *Don Juan* was not about the exploits of a seducer, nor even a moral play in the restricted sense of an edifying tale about a miscreant who comes to a bad end. In his eyes it was a play whose real subject concerns the most intensely serious issues in human life. In his words: 'it's the anguish of a man confronting his destiny: what is at stake in *Don Juan* is a man's salvation or damnation'.[9]

Jouvet's performance was totally devoid of sensuality, but suggested a remote, solitary man, sceptically contemplating the world through the filter of a cold intelligence. It was a characteristically sharp delineation from an actor renowned for the expressive precision of his gesture and corporeal attitude: his stance when he confronted the Commander (plate 1) is instantly recognisable as one of arrogant defiance. Jouvet's productions always had a strong visual impact. Part of his directorial method was a system of duplication whereby the meaning was communicated simultaneously by the words and in the visual medium. One of his dictums to his students was that 'a successful production can be seen by a blind person and a deaf person'.[10] The other striking features of the performance were Jouvet's penetratingly staccato diction and the piercing stare that seemed to transfix his victims, for example in the icy reception he gave to the succession of visitors in the fourth act. One critic wrote that it was positively terrifying to watch the 'tall silhouette, standing almost motionless, the absent, distant, weary eye that he casts on his victims like someone who is tired of the world, with sudden flashes of cruelty when he remembers that the task is not yet finished'.[11] Jouvet's tall figure was accentuated by Christian Bérard's costumes: dramatic black jacket, tights, hat and cape for the first three acts, and a flamboyant black-and-white spotted suit with balloon thighs and sleeves in the final two acts. There was nothing specifically French about these costumes. With their high flared collars they perhaps evoked a Spanish grandee, but the principal effect was not so much historical as one of high theatricality.

Plate 1 Louis Jouvet as Don Juan confronting the Statue.

With his over-weening pride, Don Juan could only be a tragic character. Jouvet carefully marked the stages of the developing tragedy, showing how he became progressively trapped in a snare of his own making. The turning point came with his encounter with the Commander. It was at this moment that the real drama began. After inspecting the Statue with scornful scepticism he lost interest in it, turned away, and told Sganarelle to invite it to supper, casually, like a black joke. But Sganarelle refused, making Don Juan repeat the order with a menacing insistence. Suddenly spectators saw, in the way the mechanism was triggered, how he was impaled on the hook of his arrogance which made it impossible for him to back down. There was another moment of profound significance when the Statue nodded its acceptance: Jouvet's face registered a moment of doubt, and there was a discernible tremor in his voice before he resumed his implacable self-assurance. From that moment onwards, it was no longer a question of defying society but of defying God.

Is Don Juan an atheist? Jouvet's answer to this vexed question was that he was not, but rather a tormented unbeliever. In one of his many Conservatoire classes devoted to the play he described him as 'a man who is searching for God, who would like to believe, but who cannot'.[12] And in another class he said: 'Don Juan is a man who does not believe, who cannot believe, and who is trying to find something to make him believe. At bottom, it's the problem everyone faces.'[13] As the last sentence implies, Jouvet was probably talking about himself here. A point which critics have understandably been reluctant to address, but which seems undeniable, is that Jouvet identified very strongly with the character he embodied in his performance. In his last years (he died in 1951) Jouvet underwent some kind of religious crisis. His productions of this period, such as Genet's *The Maids* and Graham Greene's *The Power and the Glory* (intended as his testamentary production, though he died before it opened) were pervaded with the notion of God and ideas of good and evil, themes which strongly influenced his reading of Molière's comedy. In *Don Juan*, what he presented was the portrait of a man who in Jansenist terms has not been touched by divine grace, who is condemned to go through life striving in vain to find something to justify a belief in God, and who retains his doubt up to and even at the moment of his death. That, for Jouvet, was the crucial drama of *Don Juan*. It was a powerful reading of the play, but at the same time a very personal one.

Against Jouvet's doubter, Fernand-René played Sganarelle as a simple but genuine believer. It is easy to turn Sganarelle's conformist piety to ridicule, but Fernand-René made it sincere and motivated it by linking it to the servant's devotion to his master. Departing from the tradition of the buffoonish valet, he interpreted him as a cowardly but tender man who is genuinely fearful for his reckless master's soul and who shed real tears over his grave. In Jouvet's mind, Sganarelle was a 'little brother of Saint Francis of Assisi. He has the same tenderness.'[14] The other focus of the religious theme was Elvire (Andrée Clément), a role whose beauty had haunted Jouvet for thirty years. His ideas about it were recorded in the transcription of a series of Conservatoire master-classes conducted in 1939–40, a unique documentary record of the director at work which was dramatised in Brigitte Jacques' play *Elvire Jouvet 40* in 1986. Elvire's entrance in the fourth act, he explained to the actress,

> must be surprising, supernatural. This woman who suddenly appears, unexpectedly: it must be ravishing. There is such beauty in the text, it's fluid, tender. The voice, the timbre, have to be ravishing. It's something absolutely detached, absolutely pure.[15]

Her arrival is 'a warning to Don Juan from heaven, it's the tremolo of a celestial flute; the whole speech is played in that register'.[16] Spectators had to sense that this providential warning was a miracle, an annunciation which could only be delivered by a woman transfigured by love and faith. Elvire 'loves Don Juan tenderly', she 'must be in a state of tenderness, but also of absolute detachment from the material world. There's a saintliness about her. She is a saint', he said finally.[17]

The staging, in addition to reflecting Jouvet's grandiose conception of the drama, also reveals how he aimed to stamp a structural and stylistic unity on the play. One of the problems confronting a director of Molière's *Don Juan* is its episodic structure and the associated scene changes. A strategy often adopted by directors is to follow the logic of the episodic form and present the play as a sequence of discontinuous scenes. As this has the effect of producing a more fragmented, less intense dramatic experience, it is an approach which finds favour with directors who want to distance the spectators critically from the play. Jouvet's approach went in the opposite direction. Since he intended to engage the spectators' interest in the central character's stage destiny, he needed to mould everything into a concentrated, unbroken dramatic experience. Jouvet, typically, identified this as a technical problem to which a technical solution had to be found. How could the changes of place be handled without breaking the dramatic continuity? As it happened, there was no director in France with a greater knowledge of stage machinery; he had studied its history exhaustively, but for *Don Juan* he wanted to achieve something of the fluidity of cinema without recourse to obvious machinery. If the play was not to become a machine-play spectacle at the expense of the drama, something less elaborate was needed. In the note dictated to his designer in 1945 he said: 'It would be possible to play *Don Juan* in a sequence of very simple settings on condition that they flow into each other without interruption.'[18] Following this principle, Bérard's initial designs took the motif of a forest and used it to provide the unifying theme for all the acts. He sketched a stylised forest in which the shapes could be seen both as tree-trunks and columns, and which could be modified from act to act by hanging different motifs – angels, chimera, bones or skeletons – on the trunks. When a full-scale mock-up was built on the stage of the Athénée, however, it was found that the acting space left by the forest was too restricted. Jouvet's conception of the play required a set that would allow it to breathe. Bérard returned to the drawing board and produced a more spacious setting based on a transformable set which allowed for a sequence of seven tableaux.

The basic architectural component consisted of three-storey flats rising to ten metres, with arched openings at each of the three levels. These formed a concave line marking the upstage boundary and coming down in a semi-circle to form the wings; slightly downstage, a series of different cut-out flats could be flown in. In this way, the basic structure was transformed to suggest the outside of a palace (plate 2), the arching branches of a forest, a mausoleum, an interior and so on, whilst ensuring the necessary continuity throughout the

Plate 2 Act I scene 3 of Jouvet's production (Théâtre de l'Athénée, 1947).

changing scenes. Thanks to its height and the large arched openings, the set conveyed an impressive sense of space. Jouvet was fond of saying that what counts in the theatre is height. In *Don Juan* the vertical dimension was used to provide a context for the spiritual and religious drama which he saw as the play's real subject. Just as important was the symbolic presence of the sky. The whole setting was enclosed in a semi-circular cyclorama; with no borders above or at the sides to limit it, the sky appeared boundless in the first two acts. In the subsequent acts it was partially obscured by the forest, completely masked by the interior, and then revealed again in the last act to give the backdrop of a night sky stretching to eternity.

In performance the first three acts were presented as taking place in real time, passing from morning to nightfall, with the final two acts played at night. In this way, the lighting reinforced the narrative continuity, while the gradual passage from light to darkness marked symbolically the stages of Don Juan's progression towards his confrontation with destiny.

An intrinsic part of Jouvet's initial conception was that the setting should be virtually monochrome. 'I have this idea', he explained to Bérard, 'that the play could be performed almost entirely in black and white, in settings without any real colour, and where the only colour that counts is that of the sky.'[19] The effect would be enhanced, he suggested, by purple highlights, since black, white and purple were the colours universally associated with death. In the setting that was finally used, the permanent structure was painted a neutral pale grey. The costumes were predominantly black and white. On such a scale, the effect was strikingly theatrical. Colour was then introduced by means of the lighting, using a carefully restricted range of filters.

The opening act, which took place in the early morning, started in a cool, neutral register. Jouvet specified that the sky here should have a touch of pink: not a warm pink but a harsh, unnatural pink to underline the cruel mock-voluptuousness of Don Juan's encounter with Elvire.[20] The sails of a boat in the distance provided a touch of blue for contrast. During the pastoral scenes in the second act the impression of luminosity was at its greatest. The downstage wall of the set was now removed, giving a deeper stage and allowing more of the sky to be seen. A line of clothes hung out to dry was suspended across one of the arches, in the distance was the bow of a wrecked ship, and on stage there was a small tree. Again, the stage itself was colourless except for some grass and the foliage of the tree, but the scene was permeated with the blue of the sky. In Act III, the green of the grass from the previous act was taken up as the dominant colour. Four stylised trees were placed on the stage, with more behind the arches, and some hanging greenery at the upper levels. This scene was already more sombre than the previous two. The sky was partially obscured, and oblique back-lighting darkened the greys of the upstage wall. Paradoxically, it was also the most richly coloured setting thanks partly to the dark green mass of vegetation, and also because there were indigo and purple casts in the shadows. The scene had a crepuscular atmosphere which increased as the act progressed. During the scene where Don Juan meets the mendicant the light was already fading symbolically, and the fight with the brigands and the ensuing scene with Don Carlos and Don Alonso took place at night, with shafts of moonlight striking across a shadowy stage.

The next tableau, created when the Commander's tomb loomed onto the stage towards the end of the third act, was therefore a night scene. Here Jouvet used lighting to create an eerie effect. To begin with, the scene was lit with dark, rich colouring resembling a stained-glass window, contrasting with the pale grey statue. Gradually the statue became whiter in the moonlight, and seemed to glow with phosphorescence when it invited Don Juan to dinner. The fourth act, set in Don Juan's apartment, was also played at night, with the arches in the upper storeys curtained off and the stage illuminated with candelabras. At stage-floor level, a single-storey partitioned structure had been flown in, with rectangular wings projecting downstage at each side. The various openings in the flats were heavily draped in gold brocade, so that at first spectators received the impression of a nobleman comfortably at home in a sumptuous apartment – an effect soon belied when a recessed doorway upstage centre took over as the focal point of the setting. Through this black-draped opening Monsieur Dimanche, Don Louis, Dona Elvire, and eventually the Statue, made their entrance to torment Don Juan. In the fifth act, the front wall of arches from the first act was put back in place. There was a sense of closure arising from the fact that the setting resembled that of the first act. Now, however, the cyclorama was black, and out of the shadowy recesses emerged a succession of fantastic figures: a veiled woman, a figure of Time with a scythe and a head in the form of a skull, other skeletal apparitions, and the Commander's statue.

For the final scene, which proved very controversial, Jouvet imagined a seventh tableau. The play ends with Don Juan swallowed up in hell, leaving Sganarelle asking who will pay his wages. Jouvet did not want to undermine the gravity of the death scene by staging a falsely theatrical spectacular effect with the usual accoutrements of trapdoors and flames. Nor did he see how Sganarelle could deliver his comic rejoinder without destroying the seriousness of the scene. His solution was to make Don Juan's death the climax of the play and to treat Sganarelle's last speech as a brief coda, separated in time from the main action. Thus, the scene was brought to an end at the point where Don Juan reaches out to touch the Commander's hand. Jouvet uttered a piercing cry of agony. For a moment the two figures were bathed in a phosphorescent glow while Don Juan seemed to burn from within, then the scene slowly faded to black. After a very long pause to allow this to sink in, the lights came up again on another tableau showing a baroque tomb centre-stage, with some low railings behind. The setting represented a cemetery with lighting to suggest a bright spring morning. The lid of the tomb was half-raised and the skeleton of Don Juan himself was seen in a grotesque posture as if attempting to clamber out of his tomb. Sganarelle came up to place a wreath against the tomb, contemplated his dead master, and spoke his final words in a quiet, plaintive tone. To French audiences, unaccustomed to directors taking liberties with Molière's texts, this macabre final scene was very surprising. A number of critics found it gratuitous and in bad taste. (In fact, the tomb was a meticulously researched reproduction of authentic high baroque mortuary style). But for Jouvet, this treatment was a necessary and logical way to avoid trivialising Don Juan's ultimate end. It was essential, in his eyes, that the spectators should confront the reality of Don Juan's final dissolution in death and also that they should see his fate in the context of eternity – realities too easily evaded by the play's traditional spectacular ending.

Looking at this staging, it is clear that by now Jouvet had left the lessons of Copeau and the bare stage far behind in favour of a luxurious spectacle which was curiously at odds with the privations of the winter of 1947. (On the morning of the première, one Paris newspaper catalogued the 'catastrophic economic disarray of the past three months': rising rents, falling production, commercial stagnation, and chickens at twenty times their pre-war price).[21] Instead of the reductionist absurdist drama that was starting to be produced in the little studio theatres of the Latin Quarter, Jouvet offered theatrical magnificence. It could easily have crushed the play under its weight. What saved it, no doubt, was the massive presence of Jouvet himself and the powerful metaphysical drama he communicated.

It can be objected that this single-minded but one-sided exploration of the central character eclipsed the other roles, that it devalued the master-servant relationship, or that it neglected the play's social dimension. Jouvet belonged to a school of directors who put aesthetic and humanist values before social concerns. His sole commitment was to theatre, which in practice meant to the play he was staging at the time. Ultimately, that was the key to his success with *Don Juan*, because he believed in it in a way that no one before him really had. It was not merely that he had confidence in Molière, but rather that he was passionately convinced of the theatrical qualities which, in his view, made the play a masterpiece of the first magnitude. The fact that it was reputed to be unplayable only served to increase this conviction. There was an element of defiance in his approach to *Don Juan*, as there always was in his approach to Molière. As a man of the theatre, Jouvet could never resist the challenge of demonstrating the superiority of real practitioners to critics. With reference to the low esteem in which *Don Juan* was currently held, he wrote:

> When a play, and especially one by Molière, resists analysis, that's an

> infallible sign of its interest. For anyone who has practised theatre and who also has some experience of criticism, the inability to tune in to a play is a sure sign of its merit. People who believe in Molière's genius immediately sense that they have discovered a symptom.[22]

If nothing else, the production was a vindication of this belief, overturning critical perceptions of the play as a work for the stage. After Jouvet, no critic dared to repeat the old assertions that it is a 'poorly constructed play, an unplayable role' (Sarcey), a 'badly made, disparate, incoherent play' (Faguet), or that 'strictly speaking, it is not really a work for the stage' (Gémier).

AN ATHEIST 'DON JUAN' (JEAN VILAR, DIRECTOR)

Avignon Festival, 15 July 1953

Théâtre National Populaire, 7 December 1953

It was Jouvet who ended the play's long years of purgatory and gave it the central place it subsequently came to occupy in Molière's canon. But it was Jean Vilar who gave French theatre of the middle decades of the century its definitive *Don Juan*. Mesmeric though it was, the former's production left many people feeling that it was more Jouvet than Molière. Of course, the most striking theatrical performances often are the creation of individualistic directors or leading actors (and Jouvet stamped his personality on *Don Juan* in both of these capacities). But Vilar created something more uncommon: a compelling performance of a classic which appeared simple and straightforward, not 'original' but faithful to the text, yet utterly persuasive to the point of seeming inevitable. It was often said of his productions that they restored the classics to their original freshness, and with his *Don Juan* many critics reported that they were seeing and hearing Molière's play for the first time. In fact, when French people refer to 'Vilar's *Don Juan*' it is not with the authorial sense that one speaks of 'Jouvet's *Don Juan*' or 'Planchon's *Tartuffe*'. His directorial contribution was generally perceived more in terms of overall artistic policy and choice of play rather than as the 'author' of productions. Bernard Dort wrote of his productions that 'they resist commentary, as if their sole reality was the existence they had on the stage in the presence of the public for whom they were created'.[23] The impression given was that the drama being enacted, the characters' scenic destiny, had an independent reality which eclipsed the agent that created it.

In a sense all this is misleading. His productions, and the distinctive 'style Vilar' that accompanied them, were very much the result of conscious directorial policies and choices. However, it was a style and a policy which placed great emphasis on clarity and simplicity in the interpretation of the text and which, in an age of growing directorial control, aimed to restore the creative initiative to the actors. In this respect Vilar can be seen as an inheritor of Copeau's bare stage. One key to his success as a director, then, was his faith in a great text, spoken sincerely and without mannerisms, on an empty platform.

But there was another key ingredient: the conjunction of a company of committed performers and an involved public. This, too, did not come about by accident but was the result of an astute combination of programming, audience recruitment, affordable prices and other measures designed to demystify and democratise theatre. This policy marked a significant shift in French theatre away from a concept of directing as the resolution of purely aesthetic problems and towards a more socially motivated definition of theatrical priorities.

Vilar was not the first director to pose the question of theatre's role in social terms. In 1941 Jacques Copeau, looking back on the theatrical revolution he inaugurated, wrote that 'what I now understand is that those little theatres were just technical laboratories, conservatories where the noblest dramatic traditions were nursed back to life, but which were not true theatres because they lacked a public'.[24] Aesthetically, the Cartel theatres had scaled new heights, but their audiences had been drawn from a narrow cultural elite. The real task, he now realised, was to create a theatre for the people.

After the war the three surviving members of the Cartel, Jouvet, Baty and Dullin, all devoted their last years to assisting with the movement towards decentralisation. But it was Vilar who came closer than anyone in modern times to building a truly democratic 'popular' theatre with the Avignon Festival, which he created in 1947, and the Théâtre National Populaire (TNP), which he took over in 1951. At its zenith in the 1950s, the TNP was the most successful institution of its kind in Europe. Vilar's policy of making the classics accessible to the people recruited a vast following – two million spectators, for example, between 1952 and 1957. These were theatre-goers, moreover, drawn from an unusually wide social spectrum and for whom Vilar succeeded in making the TNP a place where they felt at home. It was in this context that he produced *Don Juan*, which was performed at Avignon in the summer of 1953 and opened on the TNP's Paris stage at the Palais de Chaillot in December. The most popular of all the TNP's productions, it was given two hundred and thirty-three performances and was seen by more than a third of a million spectators, which must surely be a record for any dramatic production in pre-television days.

This was not Vilar's first experience with *Don Juan*. During the war he had directed a modest version with his first company, La Compagnie des Sept. A small independent theatre in the tradition of Copeau's Vieux-Colombier, it was dedicated primarily to modern playwrights. At this time Vilar, like Copeau, seemed to be pinning his hopes for a popular theatre on the emergence of a new vein of writing. But after a highly praised production of *Murder in the Cathedral* in 1943 he became impatient with the poverty of new plays and for his third production turned to *Don Juan*, still the least known of Molière's major works.

It was an ambitious choice which stretched the company's resources to the limit. The production, it must be admitted, was given in difficult circumstances. After a single performance for subscribers at the Vieux-Colombier on 20 April 1944, it had to transfer to the Théâtre de la Bruyère in May. Here it played for seven weeks into June, by which time most Parisians' minds were on the advancing liberation army of the Allied Forces. Because of the unreliable power supply in the final weeks of the German Occupation, the performances took place in daytime. The skylight in the roof of the theatre was uncovered and mirrors were placed at the front of the stage to reflect the available light. In Vilar's archives there is a poignant memo to the cast in which he outlined a strategy to avoid looking ridiculous in the cruel light of day: the actors should lighten their make-up, make sure their threadbare costumes were well brushed and un-creased, stay near the mirrors, and try to compensate for the production's deficiencies by the sincerity of their performance.[25]

The company's growing reputation and the unusual choice of play ensured the production attracted considerable interest, but even sympathetic critics found it hard to conceal their disappointment. Vilar himself played the title role. It was said of him that he gave a stiff, monotonous and one-dimensional portrait of the title role, and that he lacked the distinguished bearing of a 'grand seigneur'. Moreover, Vilar focused his interpretation almost exclusively on the central role, with the result that his partner Sganarelle, played by Jean Daguerre, was completely eclipsed. Vilar later declared his approach to have been erroneous, both in the interpretation of the central character and in treating the play as a single role. These were mistakes he would not repeat when he returned to the play nine years later.

At first sight there was little here that would have prepared one for his subsequent triumph in *Don Juan.* And yet, the *mise en scène,* if not the interpretation, was already founded on principles which formed the basis of all Vilar's future work. These principles were outlined in the programme notes for *Don Juan*:

> Reduce the performance to its simplest and most difficult expression, namely its interpretation by the actors. Avoid making the stage a showcase for all the major and minor arts (painting, architecture, electromania, musicomania, machinery, etc.).

> The designer's sole task: to resolve the technical requirements of discovery, surprise etc. in the simplest possible way, and to construct those scenic elements (furniture or props) which the action makes strictly indispensable.
>
> Leave mercury lamps and special effects projectors where they belong, in the music hall and circus.
>
> Limit the use of music to the introduction or linking of scenes. Only use it when it is explicitly required by the text.
>
> To summarise: eliminate all means of expression extraneous to the pure spartan laws of the stage, which demand only the interpretation of a text through the medium of the actor's body and soul.[26]

In the 1944 production these principles were not yet translated into an effective practice. The scenery, for example, consisted of some stylised branches painted on a single backcloth which was pressed into service for exterior and interior scenes alike. But the notes, amounting virtually to a credo, announce the reductive style which Vilar would perfect over the following years on the much larger stage of Avignon. In stressing the importance of the text and the actors and calling for a simplified staging which eliminated all non-essentials, Vilar placed himself clearly in the tradition of Copeau. Less obvious, but perhaps more direct, is the influence of Dullin under whom he trained in the 1930s. From his experience at Dullin's Atelier came the importance attached to simple lighting and the abhorrence of all other technical effects, especially machinery – even for a machine-play such as *Don Juan.*

When he returned to *Don Juan* as the opening production of the 1953 Avignon Festival the principle of the bare stage again dominated. But this time, on the vast platform open to the sky, the austere staging and stark lighting which in the Théâtre de la Bruyére had seemed impoverished, had the impact of a glaring truth. The empty stage represented the wide world where Don Juan and Sganarelle live

Plate 3 The stage and courtyard setting for Vilar's production in the Palais des Papes in Avignon.

out their private and public drama. The production took place in the courtyard of the Palais des Papes, a unique performance space, seemingly intimate though in fact quite a large enclosure. The action was set on two open platforms with no decor other than the high south wall with its three arched doorways behind the stage (plate 3). The only props were two tables, three chairs and a stool. The same stage arrangement was adopted for the Paris revival except that it was enclosed by the familiar black drapes which were a standard feature of TNP productions. The areas beyond the acting arena were unlit, giving the effect of a polished diamond set against a dark background. Incidental music was composed for the production by Maurice Jarre. Vilar used it sparingly, following the principles laid down earlier. Short motifs were used mainly to link scenes, but music came into play more prominently with the unearthly sound of ondes Martenot for the first meeting with the Statue in the forest, and a thunderous *Dies Irae* in the final encounter with the Statue.

When scenery was required it was created by light, the most immaterial of all scenic instruments. Vilar considered it to be invaluable because it 'increased the intensity and the cohesion of the production. And the transition to miracle and fantasy at the end is effected more easily.'[27] For example, there were two torches which, as the bearers receded into the shadows, seemed miraculously to leave their light behind on the stage. In the third act the forest was created solely by means of oblique shafts of light filtering on to the stage as if through trees. At the end of the act four widely spaced vertical columns of light were faded in to create the Commander's tomb. It was, in effect, an architecture of light which according to one critic was

> more real than a forest of real trees... In the columns of light which loom up in the dark, Don Juan and Sganarelle wander as if lost in a labyrinth, disappearing and reappearing, calling out to each other in echoing voices, brushing against the immaterial marble as they pass.[28]

These lighting effects appeared less mannered than the description might suggest because they remained secondary to the actors' imagination. It was the actors and the text ('Ah, what magnificence. Those beautiful statues. That beautiful marble! Those beautiful pillars!...') that made the imaginary scenery real.

All the effects were simple but bold. In part this reflected a moral choice within an aesthetic which equated simplicity and directness with honesty. But it should also be remembered that both at Avignon and in Paris the productions were designed for performance on large stages and to exceptionally large audiences. The theatre in the monumental Palais de Chaillot has a cavernous stage and a wide auditorium with a capacity of up to two thousand nine hundred spectators. One of Vilar's first actions when he took over the Chaillot was to bring the stage forward over the orchestra pit to create a more open playing space resembling the one in Avignon. Even so, it was an environment where fussy, elaborate detail would be futile. From setting and costume to gesture and delivery, everything had to be magnified for the drama to carry its impact to the furthermost rows of spectators. It was no doubt the demands of the space that helped Vilar to achieve the clarity of definition for which the TNP productions were famous.

What was perhaps more remarkable is that the production's limpidity was not achieved at the expense of over-simplification. By now Vilar had thoroughly revised his interpretation of the central character. Whereas in 1944 he had based his conception on the single motif of the 'grand seigneur méchant homme', the new production was a more multi-dimensional one. He recognised that the play's power lay in the challenging questions it posed rather than in the answers it gave. And of the central character he wrote: 'There is no clear explanation of Don Juan's character, let's say no "logical" or "French" explanation.'[29] Or again: 'Ten years ago the character of Don Juan threw me. He is not a monolithic character like the Miser but something more complex.'[30] This led to the high-risk strategy of composing the part without a single dominant conception. Here too the difference with Jouvet's unified Don Juan is apparent:

> I did not opt for any particular interpretation because I wanted to preserve the character's complexity. Blanchot once wrote to me that I had played one of Strindberg's characters in an 'open' way. I wanted Don Juan to be 'open'.[31]

There were very rare voices which objected that Vilar's character was incoherent – 'a touch of Tartuffe, a few drops of Richard II, a dash of Jules Berry, a hint of Machiavelli', wrote one.[32] But the impression most commonly reported was not of *a* Don Juan but the revelation of *the* Don Juan. Jacques Lemarchand voiced a common reaction when he wrote: 'The Don Juan presented by Jean Vilar seems to me to come straight out of Molière's text. It has the virtue, which frankly I have never found in any previous Don Juans, of setting spectators face to face with Molière's *Don Juan.*'[33]

This impression, again, should not be taken too literally. It may have appeared as if Don Juan was stepping to life directly out of the pages of Molière's text but in reality, of course, it was Vilar's reading that shaped the illusion. At the centre of his interpretation was the question of unbelief. Looking at the play in its cultural context, Vilar said that it was essentially a Christian subject – in the sense, that is, that the legend and the character are products of an age of strong Christian belief. And he took it as axiomatic that Molière intended his Don Juan as a disbeliever:

> It is one of the rare French plays that addresses the question of the beyond boldly and without flinching. It's wrong that in our republican schools and colleges we don't tell children that Molière did not believe in God.[34]

Accordingly, Vilar built his character around the central idea of atheism:

> Originally I played a Don Juan who believed in the existence of God. My thinking was that, if he was agnostic, why would someone as intelligent as Don Juan waste his time insulting a void? But I was mistaken, as I realised when Jean Paulhan pointed out my error. Since then I have played him as an absolute non-believer.[35]

Don Juan's costume, designed by Vilar's usual collaborator Léon Gischia, was not Spanish or Sicilian but represented a swash-buckling French musketeer who was more Louis XIII than Louis XIV (plate 4). The elaborate ornamentation described by Pierrot to Charlotte was simplified. With high lace collar, knee-length boots, plumed hat and sword, it seemed a suprising choice at first. But it fitted Vilar's conception of the character as a bold free-thinker by evoking a Cartesian rationalist and avoiding connotations of a courtier of the more cynical mid-century Louis XIV period. For there was no blasé insincerity in Vilar's Don Juan, as was made clear in the crucial hypocrisy scene. The famous tirade was not spoken to

Plate 4 Daniel Sorano (Sganarelle) and Jean Vilar (Don Juan) at the TNP, 1953.

Sganarelle but delivered directly to the audience in a boldly declamatory style. In this way Vilar, who probably considered Don Juan to be Molière's spokesman here, made it clear that the set-piece speech had the force of universal satire.

This was not, then, the 'wicked nobleman' of his first production, nor a libertine poseur such as Meyerhold envisaged him, but a character, like Jouvet's Don Juan, who is responsible for the weight of his thought and actions. But to make a further distinction, whereas Jouvet showed a Don Juan tormented by the quest for a God who is never revealed, Vilar shifted the focus from the spiritual drama to the philosophical consequences of his atheism, as the following remark implies: 'Molière makes him an atheist, that is certain. Or, as they said at the time, a 'libertin' – the latin word, you see. *Liber.*'[36] The central issue which the production raised was the problem of man's freedom in a world without God. It showed Don Juan exploring the limits of his freedom to the utmost. Not that Vilar saw the character's solution as being necessarily correct. It was the fact that the play raised burning questions about man's social responsibilities that made it such a pertinent choice for the repertoire of a contemporary popular theatre. *Don Juan*, said Vilar,

> is the most modern of all Molière's works, the one which comes nearest to our thinking, our anxieties, our beliefs, our moral outlook... For a popular public the character of Don Juan poses fundamental questions about relations between father and son, husband and wife. This is not to say his answers are the right ones to follow. Moreover, his attitude towards a bond of words (Don Carlos), towards false generosity (the Beggar), towards money (M. Dimanche) is quite surprising.[37]

While the last quotation indicates the general areas Vilar wished to explore, it would be no easy matter to say what lesson he wanted spectators to draw. Although his purpose was to direct attention to the play's social dimensions, it was in no sense a didactic production nor even a 'political' production in the usual sense of the term. Vilar's political stance – leftist, republican, and committed to a civic ideal of cultural mission – permeated his entire work, but it expressed itself indirectly. Its primary instrument was the repertoire, where Vilar looked for plays which implicitly shed light on contemporary social and political questions. As a director, however, he always maintained that his role was not to interpose a personal interpretation between the text and the spectator. He disliked the title *metteur en scène* ('director') and preferred to be known as a *régisseur*. What this implied was that he saw his role in terms of organising optimum conditions for the text to be communicated to the public through the medium of the performers. Which, in turn, implied a belief that, if a play was relevant, it should be allowed to speak for itself: 'Convince, without subjugating the play. Illuminate it, not dress it up. Without vulgarising it, make it beautiful and accessible to everyone.'[38] All this added up to a programme which aimed to stimulate critical reflection without directing audiences to specific responses. Such an approach led to the director of the TNP being criticised from the right for politicising a state institution (as if it could be anything other than political!), and attacked even more fiercely from the left (notably by Sartre) for his perceived betrayal of people's theatre. But it was also the approach which made productions like *Don Juan* accessible and popular to an unprecedented degree.

So there was nothing formulaic about his *Don Juan*. For Roland Barthes what gave the production its contemporary significance was the heroic affirmation of Don Juan's atheism. Barthes argued that previous readings of the play had adopted the comforting bourgeois strategy of treating the subject as the illustration of a purely local, historical atheism. In contrast, he said, Vilar 'brings Don Juan out from the ghetto of anecdote and gives him a biological consistency so that every night two thousand astonished spectators receive the full force of it in their chest'.[39] What he gave, Barthes continued, was not the psychology of an atheist but the 'biology' of an atheist, that is to say a man who is an atheist not in his speech but in his fibres. And in his silences. Vilar had noticed that at certain key moments – in response to Sganarelle's questioning, for example, or at the sight of the nodding Statue – Don Juan remains silent. Rather than treating the silences as equivocation, he charged them with positive expressive power. In Barthes' words: 'Vilar's silence is the silence not of a man who doubts but of a man who knows. His Don Juan is not so much deprived of belief as endowed with certainty.'[40]

Obviously, Vilar did not intend the hero's death to be seen as a symbol of divine punishment. He said: 'Don Juan's downfall and death are dealt with in a rapid conjuring trick. It cannot be seen as exactly seriously.'[41] So the Statue, plaster-like and excessively solid, seemed to proclaim its own artificiality and the death scene was handled simply with no pyrotechnic effects. Defiant to the end, Don Juan put his hand in the Commander's and collapsed instantly. The traditional image of a body consumed in the fire of hell was replaced by the impression of a man electrocuted, or possibly suffering a heart attack. He lay rigidly on his back with clenched fists and bulging eyes, looking, as one critic memorably put it, 'like the stiff corpse of a bird which had impudently perched on a high voltage cable and fallen to earth like a stone'.[42]

What is being described here is a mature conception which Vilar did not arrive at straight away. Just as he revised his conception of the play as a result of the 1944 production, so his performance at the TNP was modified in the light of experience gained in Avignon. The commonly received impression given by the latter was of a man struggling to break the bonds of belief. Georges Lerminier saw 'a troubled, tormented Don Juan, a man who has wagered against God and sticks to his bet with proud, provocative stubbornness'.[43] Robert Kemp saw a haunted man: 'Don Juan is afraid. Afraid of error, afraid of Hell, afraid of God whom he denies to reassure himself. Beneath Don Juan's sarcastic manner, Vilar's gestures and face give a hint of a possible conversion.'[44] A future conversion was almost certainly not what Vilar intended to suggest. For the Chaillot revival his interpretation was sharpened with perceptible benefits. Kemp now wrote that 'in July I had the impression in the second part that Vilar made Don Juan hesitate in his atheism. After his first encounter with the Statue he seemed unsettled, persisting only out of stubborn pride'. But now, he said, 'Don Juan resists more.'[45] For Jacques Lemarchand the development was even more marked:

> In the summer production his Don Juan was more a Christian in revolt than an unbeliever. His courage as he battled against a God who, he knew from the start, would have the last word, was moving. The Don Juan he shows us now is more settled and more terrible. He is certain – with the certainty of an inner conviction which nothing will prevail against – that he is, and will be, answerable to no one.[46]

Vilar continued to harden the atheism throughout the play's many revivals. The production gained not only in clarity but also in its power of provocation. Don Juan's open scorn for conventional morality, his flagrant indifference to the harm he causes, and the conscious sadism that many observers felt (for example in his treatment of the Beggar) became all the more unanswerable in the light of his resolute atheism.

The other major change concerned Sganarelle's role. Having focused his first production on Don Juan, Vilar realised, as most directors discover, that the play is built around an indissoluble couple. Productions which treat the servant only as a sounding board for the master's thoughts and feelings tend to be unstable, since they deprive Don Juan of the buttressing contrary force that enables him to find his own true weight. Moreover, the structural balance of the play as a whole depends on the counter-weight provided by the ever-present Sganarelle. (He is, in fact, on stage during all but one of the play's twenty-seven scenes, more than Don Juan himself). In his new production Vilar treated Sganarelle as the embodiment of the master's alter ego, and tried to highlight the symbiotic nature of the two characters: 'Sganarelle is Don Juan's double. Or, more exactly, they are two aspects of the same satire, of the same critical idea.'[47]

Daniel Sorano was an ideal actor for the role. One of the mainstays of the TNP until his untimely death in 1959, he was a remarkable comic actor who also had a powerful sense of the ensemble. His performance was generally considered the most successful modern interpretation of the role. Its immediate appeal sprang from the way Sorano exploited the elemental comic resources of the role – naivety, cowardice and incredulity – to the full. His costume was modelled on a traditional servant's outfit worn by Molière (see plate 4), and Vilar encouraged him to play with the vitality and boldness associated with Molière's troupe, with acrobatic movements and broad facial gestures. However, it was not a virtuoso solo number but was closely moulded to Vilar's Don Juan. A feature which was much remarked upon was the extraordinary intensity of Sorano's participation in the action. What spectators saw was, in Bernard Dort's words, 'not a mere master-servant relationship but a complicity, a hateful intimacy. At every moment and in every situation, alone and face to face, Don Juan is Sganarelle's demon, and Sganarelle the judge and sole witness of Don Juan.'[48]

The encouragement to Sorano to act boldly also governed Vilar's advice to the cast as a whole. Already, with his first production of *Don Juan*, he had identified a general approach to Molière. In a note dated 3 May 1944 he wrote to the cast: 'On the whole the so-called comic scenes are being taken too quickly. They lack weight. They need more emphasis.' And, making an interesting distinction, he advised: 'Do not play Molière in what you imagine to be the style of the Italian players but in the great earthy French style.'[49] It is sometimes forgotten that there was a native tradition of French farce, less stylised than the more familiar *commedia dell'arte.* In Vilar's mind the Italian tradition evidently meant light and graceful (as it became in the eighteenth century), whereas what Molière required was, in addition and above all, robustness. In other words: in the spirit of Rabelais not Marivaux.

As well as vigour, the acting tended towards a demonstrative style. Vilar's own acting method, like Jouvet's, had an analytical core.

Embracing the character without totally identifying with it, he maintained sufficient distance between himself and the character to introduce a slight note of irony. Vilar himself gave the impression of simultaneously living and creating the character in the moment of performance. Referring to his 'infinitely nuanced portrait', Georges Lerminier said: 'He paints it before our eyes, as if playing himself.'[50] Another wrote that 'Vilar illuminated and explained the character's multiple nuances by decomposing all its facets in the prism of a penetrating analysis. And, moreover, without this prodigious decomposition robbing the character of its innermost shadows. The character is exposed in glaring light, but retains all its consistency.'[51] Brecht's work was known to Vilar who in 1951 had been the first stage *Mother Courage* in France. At that time, however, the Berliner Ensemble had not yet visited France (that happened in 1954) and Brecht's ideas, in particular his staging techniques, were not well understood. But Vilar seems instinctively to have been coming close to a Brechtian distancing effect. How far he imposed this on other members of the cast is hard to judge. Vilar was famous for the trust he placed in his actors. His rehearsal method, which one actress described as more 'conditioning' than 'directing', was rather to prompt performers towards their own grasp of the roles. But they were certainly encouraged to come downstage and address the audience. Like Don Juan's hypocrisy tirade, two other key speeches – Sganarelle's parody of reasoning and Elvire's fourth-act appeal for repentance – were also delivered beyond Don Juan directly to the spectators.

Many of these impressions can be verified by listening to a recording of the performance, made at the Palais de Chaillot in 1954. There is a telling absence of mannerisms. It is clearly the work of a company who are confident that they only have to speak Molière's words honestly for their full impact to be felt. The measured pace, for which some of his productions were criticised, is also there. This special delivery was partly a function of the size of the stage, which required bold movements, and the auditorium, where the words had to carry their resonance to the distant back rows. Very slow at the beginning, the performance preserves an *in lento* delivery to the end despite some quickening of pace in the more physical scenes in the second and fourth acts when Don Juan meets the villagers and Elvire's brothers. But the slow pacing soon comes to sound right and the most lasting impression, paradoxically, is of a steady, relentless momentum.

Vilar's production was seen as the definitive *Don Juan* of the decade and left a lasting mark on the play. Two factors were principally responsible for this. One was the denuded clarity of the staging which inspired one critic to proclaim:

> There will come a day when theatre historians will hail this *Don Juan* as an example. On the one hand they will decry all the stage trickery of earlier years, all the enormous efforts that were expended on taming this dark masterpiece, all the absurd, simplistic baroquery – when, for example, one saw the curtain fall and rise again to show Sganarelle crying over his master's papier-mâché tomb. And on the other hand, they will evoke the consummate mastery with which Vilar links all the scenes and fuses them in a supreme harmony.[52]

The other factor which made *Don Juan* a keystone of the TNP's repertoire was the special resonance which Vilar gave to the subject in the context of the popular theatre movement. Rather than presenting a myth it explored a social problem. It presented spectators with a character who was neither a monster nor a superman but a courageous, wrong-headed individualist through whom they vicariously explored the limits of their own freedom. And who reminded them of their responsibilities in a world where they are totally free.

A MARXIST 'DON JUAN' (PATRICE CHÉREAU, DIRECTOR)

Théâtre du Huitième, Lyon, 3 January 1969

The scenic revolution which shaped the priorities of French theatre between the wars was based on a concept of staging as an aesthetic operation governed by a system of values based on taste, beauty and emotion. A major change that occurred in France during the 1950s was the replacement of this artistic system by a social definition of theatre's purpose. In a desire to bring theatre closer to the sphere of political reflection, many directors came to regard their task as an exercise in critical staging. It was through Brecht's example and, in several cases, by literal copying of his methods, that they acquired a scenic language to express these concerns.

A key mediator between Brecht and the French stage was Roger Planchon. During the 1950s, at the Théâtre de la Cité in Villeurbanne, Planchon was the first French director fully to embrace Brecht. It was by studying Brecht's productions that he became conscious of the social responsibility of directing and formulated the notion of 'scenic writing' as a method of critical reflection upon the text. Regarding the classical repertoire, which came to play an increasingly central role in directorial experiments during the 1960s, Planchon also wrote: 'It was [Brecht's] influence that led me to read the classics. He insisted on the basic importance of understanding the heritage of the past. I realised I had not read the French classics.'[53]

One consequence of these developments was a profound shift in the way directors perceived their relationship with the play. The Cartel directors, conceiving their role as servants of the play, referred to 'fidelity' to the text as the ultimate justification of their staging operations. Their aim was always to express the 'spirit' of the play: not to explain it from a detached viewpoint but to espouse the text – listening to it without preconceptions, being receptive to the rhythms and style of the writing, attuning themselves to the source of its inspiration. In contrast to this, the method which Planchon calls *mise en scène critique* is an objectively critical process whose purpose is not to reveal an essence but to historicise the text. As Brecht said of the classics:

> The important thing is to play works of the past in a historical manner, that is to say, to place them in strong opposition to our own age. It is only against the backcloth of our age that their form appears old, and I doubt whether, without this backdrop, their meaning can be revealed at all.[54]

The aim of Marxist directors like Planchon when approaching classical texts has thus been to stage a reading which situates them in its historical and social context, and to represent this totality for a modern-day audience. Or, as Bernard Dort has written,

> [such productions] aim not only to represent what Stanislavsky called the sub-text (i.e. the deep psychological reality underlying the characters' spoken words) but also the 'supra-text', namely their social environment seen in a historical perspective (our perspective: that of spectators in the late twentieth century).[55]

The first Brechtian staging of a play by Molière in France was *George Dandin*, produced by Planchon in 1958. Dort, the most influential left-wing theatre critic in France of the last thirty years, instantly recognised its importance and concluded his review with the prescient statement that with this single production Planchon 'opens up a new path for a new usage of our classics'.[56] In the event it was not so much a path as the major highway, at least until the post-1968 disillusionment set in and directors began to favour de-constructing reality rather than explaining it historically. Planchon's *George Dandin* inspired a wave of experiment as directors set about mining the classics – and above all Molière – for their ideological significance. Patrice Chéreau's *Don Juan* (1969) is one of a number of productions of the play which derive from the process set in train by Planchon. Others that could be mentioned are the productions by Bernard Sobel (a former pupil of Brecht), Michel Humbert and Planchon's own *Don Juan*. Boutté's production at the Comédie-Française, discussed in the following section, is a more distant derivative. Chéreau's has been chosen for discussion here as the most distinctive and influential exemplar of this genre. Together with Planchon's *Tartuffe* (1963 and 1973), it was one of the landmark productions of Molière in recent decades.

Chéreau himself, the son of a painter and a textile designer, had an academic background in music and design when he first became involved with an amateur theatre group at the Lycée Louis-le-Grand in Paris. A series of productions of little-known classics earned him an invitation from the Marxist director Bernard Sobel to mount his first professional production at the latter's municipal theatre in the working-class suburb of Gennevilliers. Its success led to Chéreau being appointed director of the theatre at Sartrouville, a small dormitory town ten miles north-west of Paris, in 1966. His final piece of work at Sartrouville in 1969 was *Don Juan*, a co-production with Marcel Maréchal's Compagnie du Cothurne in Lyon. Premièred in Lyon at the Théâtre du Huitième, and later transferred to Sartrouville, it revealed Chéreau at the age of twenty-five as one of France's most original, if most disputed, interpreters of the classics.

Chéreau's subsequent career has been a succession of always controversial productions which have brought international acclaim. A period of freelance directing in France and Italy came to an end in 1973 when Planchon, accepting the directorship of the TNP in Villeurbanne, appointed Chéreau his co-director. At the age of twenty-eight he thus came to the head of a major national stage where he remained until moving on to the Théâtre des Amandiers in Nanterre in 1982. Chéreau has mounted provocative productions of Shakespeare (*Richard II*: Marseilles and Paris, 1970), Wedekind (*Lulu*: Piccolo Teatro, Milan, 1971), Marlowe (*The Massacre at Paris*: Paris, 1972), Ibsen (*Peer Gynt*: 1981) and Genet (*The Screens*: 1983). When he turned his attention to opera the results were even more sensational. His production of Wagner's *Ring* cycle with Pierre

Boulez (Bayreuth, 1976–80), in which the Nordic legends were transcribed in stunning images of the industrial revolution, left the Bayreuth establishment and many German opera critics reeling.

Don Juan was the first major exemplar of these 'concept productions': powerful theatrical transcriptions of ideologically inspired readings of the text. They reflect Chéreau's conception of his directorial role as the expression of a social commitment. 'The essential thing', he said when preparing *Don Juan*, 'is to take a political position, but above all a moral position: you have to show, from your own moral standpoint, how you read the story, which elements you are going to privilege, how you interpret the choices made by the characters.'[57] Whilst this approach is not in itself original, what distinguishes his productions is the strength of his grasp when he seizes a play. Its hallmarks are a reading of the play which is rigorously coherent if sometimes one-sided, coupled with highly charged and impeccably executed stage imagery. After Brecht, his acknowledged masters in modern theatre are Planchon and Strehler, and his own productions could be said to combine Planchon's critical staging techniques with the latter's stunning visual qualities. A scenographer first and foremost rather than a director of actors, Chéreau designs his own productions, usually in collaboration with his assistant Richard Péduzzi. And although he has occasionally taken walk-on parts, unlike virtually every French director before him he is not an actor by calling. It should not be concluded from this that he systematically works to diminish the actor's contribution to the overall theatrical concept. In fact, his actors are more than ciphers and his work depends very much on their human presence for its success. It is the case, however, that his productions are very markedly those of a scenographer who uses settings as the main signifying component of the production. Long after the production is over, Chéreau's stage pictures remain lodged in the mind: images of peasants as in a winter scene from a painting by Le Nain, of ant-like masses toiling in a bleak industrial landscape, or of Siegfried forging his sword with a giant steam hammer.

In *Don Juan*, as in many of his productions, the over-arching concept was of the stage as a *machine à jouer* ('acting machine'), a non-representational scenic construction in which a theatrical performance was seen to be given. With Molière's play the word 'machine' actually has a literal and historical significance, for the play itself is a seventeenth-century machine-play. Chéreau took this idea as a metaphor for the play's ideological discourse and equipped the stage with machinery operated by actors who were, in effect, seen to be controlling the mechanism by which the play was represented.

Before looking at the way this staging worked it will be helpful to consider the historical analysis – the 'supra-text' – as Chéreau conceived it. In a special issue of the journal of the Compagnie du Cothurne devoted to *Don Juan* he outlined the political reality that the play attests to. In 1665 France had recently experienced a violent civil war. The Fronde was the final spasm of a feudal nobility attempting to re-assert its traditional independence against the growing powers of the throne, and its suppression signalled the emasculation of the old ruling class. At the moment when Molière was writing, a new political order of centralised monarchy was thus being consolidated under the young King, his patron. It was against this background that Molière turned his attention in *Don Juan* to the old feudal nobility struggling to come to terms with the new political reality. Don Louis' nostalgia for the past, the way he identifies his son's abandonment of aristocratic honour as the cause of the temporal decline of his class, Don Carlos' adherence to an outmoded chivalrous code which leads him to turn his violence against his brother instead of their common enemy: all these things reflect the confusion of individuals caught up in a historical process which they neither control nor fully understand.

Within their ranks stands an individualist – Don Juan. Profiting from the disintegrating feudal system, the young aristocrat interiorises his aristocratic privilege to invent his own 'art of living', a materialistic code in which personal pleasure is sovereign. In Chéreau's eyes, Don Juan's adventure is both negative and positive:

> Positive, because of his moral independence and his eroticism and because, as a progressive and a traitor to his own class, he works to erode the old feudal world from within. Negative because he experiences History in the form of an egocentric adventure, and because he needs the old order in order to live.[58]

Ultimately, Chéreau suggested, Don Juan is a progressive who is trapped in the contradictions of his own position. 'Don Juan imagines himself as a builder; in fact, he is used by others to perform some demolition work inside his own class.'[59] He is not so much a triumphant immoralist but 'a sort of intellectual who has very few means at his disposal for changing the world and who, in the end, prefers to change himself. It's a form of intellectual cowardice.'[60] (Chéreau implied, moreover, that the ambiguity of his position mirrored that of left-wing bourgeois intellectuals in the uprising of May 1968).

No less fascinating is what the play reflects of Molière's position in relation to the society of his time. In the article mentioned above, Chéreau also wrote:

> In the face of this emergent order, Molière adopts a marvellous ambiguity: on the one hand objective defender of the dominant ideology, and on the other hand 'realistic visionary', inventor of a fable and precise narrator. *Don Juan,* more than any other play, bears witness to this ambiguity. While attacking the enemies of the regime in the form of a machine-play, the play gives an exact account of the conflicts in contemporary society and a vivid picture of the problems faced by an individual in trying to live his own life.[61]

At one level the play poetically dramatises the characters' personal experience, showing how their lives are shaped by ideological conflict at a particular historical moment. This is Molière the 'realistic visionary'. At another level, the play itself is an ideological statement in which Molière acknowledges the new political order, a fact which is reflected in his adoption of a machine-play to recount the suppression of his troublesome hero. Chéreau suggests that we should not be deceived by the *deus ex machina* into viewing the subject as a mystical play. In fact, he says, *Don Juan* is 'the opposite of a mystical play', one where the supernatural is 'an ideological cloak':

> Don Juan's death and the appearance of the Commander are nothing other than an ideological discourse inviting us to join in the euphoric celebration of the enemy's moral annihilation.[62]

In other words, the machine-play becomes, literally, a machine for killing libertines. The production made this very clear in the manner of Don Juan's death which was stripped of its mystical attributes and presented as a brutally mechanical operation. The Commander was no miracle but a hideous, bulky machine in grey plaster operated by stagehands. At the dénouement instead of one statue there were now two, which bore down on Don Juan like automata, punching and crushing him to death.

These reflections on the supra-text were expressed metaphorically in the performance space which Chéreau conceived for the production (plate 5). It combined an inner and an outer stage, creating a play-within-the-play. The play itself was performed on a platform stage with its own décor. Surrounding it, in towers rising up to left and right of the proscenium and in the pit below the open front of the main stage, there was a system of primitive machinery of the kind illustrated in antique encyclopedias. Six actors wearing rags remained crouched at the front of the stage throughout the performance, watching the play or sleeping on straw until a whistle roused them to work. Then they operated the winching handles, whereupon the pulleys and chains, cogs, winding drums and counterweights were seen to drive the revolving stage, change the scenery, or make the Statue move.

The principal action was performed on a platform stage with a cobbled surface and a revolve in the floor for scene changes. Along the back of the stage was placed a cut-out facade of the Place Royale, but on a strangely miniaturised scale. On an empty stage it presented the illusion of a distant glimpse of Louis XIV's Paris seen in a receding perspective. As soon as the actors were present on the stage,

Plate 5 View of the stage for Chéreau's production at Sartrouville, 1969.

however, they appeared to be towering over a row of dolls' houses whose dwarfed proportions revealed the cut-out as a piece of theatrical *trompe-l'œil.* A full-width cyclorama formed the upstage boundary. While the perspective remained in place throughout the performance, giving a permanent but symbolically remote evocation of the aristocratic milieu, two movable sets were placed in front of it. The first, used in Acts I and IV, was Don Juan's 'palace' – in reality, the bare shell of an abandoned farm or manor house, with grass growing out of ruined stone walls. The delapidated manor house could be construed as suggesting the collapse of the feudal system. Its other function was to underline Don Juan's position as a class traitor which was represented, in Chéreau's production, by showing him living literally as an outlaw. The second scenic element was the Commander's tomb, a three-storey Palladian structure of which only one wing was complete initially. Having cranked it into place at the end of the third act, the machine-operators swarmed over ladders to continued the building, a process which resumed again at the end of the play. Thus, as Don Juan's ancient refuge was falling into ruins, a new classical edifice proclaiming triumphant Christianity was seen to rise in its place.

All this was very remote from the traditional Sicilian seashore and forests, reflecting Chéreau's desire to wrench the text from the legend and re-situate it in its theatrical and historical context. A central feature of the production concept was the role that it gave to a whole social class – the common labourers – which in the play itself is consigned to a passive role. In the parallel commentary which Chéreau constructed around the play they had an active role, for it was the actors on the stage floor who permitted the play to be performed by operating the machinery. As a symbol of the fifteen million anonymous peasants who constituted three quarters of Louis XIV's subjects in 1665, their political alienation was conveyed in the way that their function was to act as executants of the 'machine for killing libertines'. It was also they who supplied the final image. When the action was finished, they took over the stage and continued building the Commander's tomb, giving the impression, perhaps, of appropriating the future for themselves.

A striking feature of the production was the climate of physical violence in which it was performed. 'I want to show how the parties involved in a struggle for a better life are embodied in the most concrete, brutal fashion', said Chéreau in 1968.[63] Fascinated by the individual's experience of conflict in societies in a state of mutation, he staged *Don Juan* in a way which highlighted the opposition between the individual and the collective which lies at the root of most drama. Penetrating the surface of social interaction to identify the power struggles that lie beneath, he used naked aggression and brute force to externalise the underlying conflict. The attitudes struck by the actors were menacing or wary, encounters became skirmishes or outright fights. It was noticeable that the fights involved no swords, only hand-to-hand combat to underline the primitive nature of the power struggle.

A similar mechanism was seen in the presentation of the characters, who were shown to fall into opposing interest-groups, each defined by their style of costume and the various extras who accompanied them. The theme of pursuit is, of course, one of the unifying mechanisms of Molière's plot. Chéreau brought it to the fore, making it a central idea of the play and expressing it visually in concrete motifs. He said that he saw the action as 'a sort of Western'[64] and in outline it was possible to discern the classic Western structure of a renegade outlaw being tracked down by members of his old gang who have formed a group of vigilantes to exact revenge. The key accessory in the production was a hand-cart. In the first act Don Juan's men were loading it with trunks and cases, ready for the off. During the course of the performance it accompanied Don Juan and Sganarelle on their peregrinations and came to symbolise the central character's outlawed status.

Every production detail was thus subordinated to the central idea that the play recounts the ideological liquidation of Don Juan. Chéreau also used a number of extras to mark the alignment of forces. Elvire's brothers had a following of 'heavies', grotesquely padded up like baseball players. Don Juan himself was accompanied by three 'servants' – actually unshaven ruffians who behaved on stage like members of his gang. In the first act where Don Juan proffers insincere explanations of his sudden departure to Elvire, they watched with their arms folded in silent mockery, relishing her humiliation; in the scene between Don Juan and the hermit they joined in to taunt the old man. The opposition of forces was further underlined by the actors' contrasting bulk and physical appearance. The slim figure of Don Juan (Gérard Guillaumat) in a supple leather suit, looked vulnerable but agile, ready for flight. Elvire's brothers appeared in a very striking and unexpected guise, dressed in enormous hairy animal skins which made them resemble Siberian hunters. Don Juan's father was similarly dressed. When he came to rebuke his reprobate son in the fourth act he stood like a prehistoric creature bellowing, rather than speaking, his monarchist tirade.

The point of Chéreau's approach is that it is not primarily a study of characters but of situations and actions, through which it is revealed how each individual's behaviour is affected by the social and ideological framework of his or her life. Speaking of *Don Juan*, Chéreau said: 'When you examine it closely there is something incoherent about the play. The spoken words actually conceal the characters' inner motivation and objectives, their precise relationships, their real thoughts. Behind the fine language, what exactly is going on at each moment? That's what intrigued us.'[65] Chéreau's direction of the actors was concerned with externalising the inner processes though amplified gestures. None of the characters escaped this demystifying scrutiny. Elvire's dignified verbal remonstrations to Don Juan in the first act, for example, were seen as a mask for her seething frustration. The actress Roséliane Goldstein communicated this through unconstrained hysteria, writhing at the feet of her former lover and clutching his legs, and eventually collapsing into unconsciousness. In the fourth act her sexual frustration was sublimated into a tearful and trance-like spiritual ecstasy.

Described bluntly, these techniques sound somewhat crude but in the context and climate of the production they fitted exactly into a coherent overall reading of the play. One critic wrote:

> However systematically provocative they seem, virtually all [Chéreau's] ideas eventually appear justified. It becomes normal to see Don Juan reduced to the status of the leader of a cynical, puerile gang, and Elvire as a hysterical adolescent drunk on mysticism, just as it becomes normal to see Charlotte and Pierrot and the Beggar voicing the genuine torment of the underdog. After all, why must Charlotte's seduction always be played with merry laughter amid drying laundry?[66]

The peasant scenes referred to here gave rise to some of the most original and powerful moments of the performance. Chéreau presented them with unprecedented force in a manner totally unlike the traditional pastoral. They took place on an empty stage, with only the distant view of Louis XIV's Paris in the background and the hand-cart for a prop. Bernard Ballet's Pierrot was a tragic clown skilfully performing pirouettes for an unappreciative Charlotte. His extreme awkwardness in verbal expression signalled his alienation and marked him out as an inevitable social victim. Pierrot takes delight in recounting to Charlotte how he has tricked a fellow-peasant out of money – a detail which is often glossed over, but which was carefully highlighted in Chéreau's production as it betrayed the speaker's tragic lack of class awareness. Charlotte's indifference to her suitor's complaints, her unconcealed boredom at the narration of his life-saving escapade, and her sudden erotic arousal when Pierrot described Don Juan's aristocratic attire, were all painful to witness. The seduction of this easy prey by Don Juan was excrutiating. As the nobleman languidly went through his practised routine, Charlotte gave herself to him in total self-abandon, panting excitedly under Don Juan's fondling hands. Even the hardened Sganarelle, in the role of proxy audience to the scene, could not bear to watch the climax and covered his ears with his hands. Pierrot's return brought another painful scene. With relentless precision Chéreau laid bare the successive phases of a primeval power struggle: the two males measuring each other up, the female siding with the stronger male, the physical beating of the weaker male and his humiliated withdrawal. The fourth scene, when Charlotte's rival re-appears, brought the further episode of the two females fighting for possession of the male victor, and the sight of Don Juan relishing the spectacle as they rolled on the floor furiously pummelling and clawing each other.

An act which has seemed an incidental episode to many a director, or at best an amusing display of peasant naivety, thus became one of the production's high points. One commentator spoke of its 'unbearable realism' and went on to say:

> Never in any production of *Don Juan* has this second act (which so often seems folkloric, with its peasant patois) been revealed as it is here, in all its brutal truth: an appalling, almost intolerable, documentation of the alienation and the brutalising condition of the oppressed classes in the lingering feudal society of the seventeenth century.[67]

The eternal counterpart to the master is of course the servant. Another of the production's distinctive contributions was its handling of the relationship between the two main characters. Traditionally, their relationship is seen as a symbiotic and complementary one, either representing contrasting attitudes to belief (Jouvet), or expressing human solidarity (Vilar), or incarnating two versions of the same existential experience (Bourseiller's *Don Juan*, discussed in the following chapter). In all those productions Sganarelle's function, within the terms of their overall conceptual framework, is to act as Don Juan's alter ego. Chéreau implied that the idea of the loyal servant bonded to the master is a comforting bourgeois deception. Considered in class terms, the only bond that ties the servant to the master is economic necessity. This production dramatised a progressive deterioration in their relationship, a development which perhaps hinted at an eventual awakening of class consciousness on Sganarelle's part. If there seemed initially to be some complicity between the two that went beyond the obvious nexus of wages, Gérard Guillaumat as Don Juan suggested that this was because he was attempting to create it for his own benefit. But during the course of the performance, and particularly in the last two acts, there was a perceptible hardening of Sganarelle's attitude towards his master. This process has a basis in Molière's text where Sganarelle is increasingly scandalised by each new moral outrage committed by Don Juan. Chéreau merely drew a sociological lesson from the fact and pursued it to its logical conclusion. So whereas in Vilar's and Jouvet's productions Sganarelle stuck by his master through thick and thin, Chéreau's showed how it was increasingly impossible for him to follow Don Juan. 'At the end', he said, 'they are nothing to each other. Except perhaps someone who pays and someone who wants to be paid.'[68]

It was this concern with the master-servant relationship, apparently, that led to the omission of the scene where Don Juan is visited by M. Dimanche. To many people it seemed an extraordinary omission, and particularly puzzling in a Marxist-inspired interpretation since the tradesman creditor provides the only representative within the play of the ascendant class which would one day displace the dying aristocracy. But Chéreau said the decision to cut the scene, which was not one that was originally planned, sprang from another concern. He explained:

> I did not intend to cut it initially. We spent a lot of time rehearsing it in different ways and with different actors. But it was no good. From the perspective we had adopted there was something indecipherable about the scene... It was getting in the way at a stage in the action where what mattered for us above all was hardening the relationship between Don Juan and Sganarelle.[69]

As for Sganarelle himself, Chéreau envisaged him as 'a blind creature who possesses only the tragic awareness of his own lack of understanding, but he is indestructible and so one day will enjoy strength and power'.[70] The real progenitor of Sganarelle, however, was not the director but the actor Marcel Maréchal. It was Maréchal who, as director of the Théâtre du Huitième in Lyon, had suggested to Chéreau the idea of a co-production, attracted by the latter's growing reputation and their shared ideological outlook. He was also stimulated by the very real artistic challenge involved in the conjunction of his own acting style – warm, generous and corporeal – with Chéreau's more cerebral, analytical approach. Leaving the security of his own company he went to join Chéreau's in Sartrouville where the early rehearsals plunged him into despair. The director's 'archaeological' method, as Maréchal called it, seemed to be crushing the actors' personalities. But, he said, 'very soon I learned how to resist effectively, how to serve our future spectacle with my own contribution... I learned to shut my ears to Chéreau's archaeological readings of the text, the better to give my body to the quest for Sganarelle... From that moment, the work began to advance. Instead of a sulky resister I became a jubilant dynamiter.'[71]

Maréchal's extraordinary Sganarelle (plate 6), interpreted as a poignant Chaplinesque clown with a battered hat, met with unanimous critical acclaim. The actor's personal qualities infused a devastating human reality into a character who might easily have become a cipher. And instead of clashing with the director's reading, his interpretation supplied the necessary complement to Chéreau's. It was as if, from two different starting points, one historical the other inner, Chéreau and Maréchal projected conceptions which fused to produce a three-dimensional character. Maréchal said that what he played was

> the tragedy of a man of the people who does not have access
> to language, and therefore to culture, and therefore to liberty...
> A brilliant proletarian and individualist, he knows instinctively
> that whoever commands language commands power.[72]

In Act I scene 2, Don Juan gives Sganarelle permission to speak and asks him if he has anything to say, to which the latter can only reply: 'Yes, what I've got to say is ... I don't know what to say.' In the third act, Sganarelle's attempt at reasoning produces a flood of

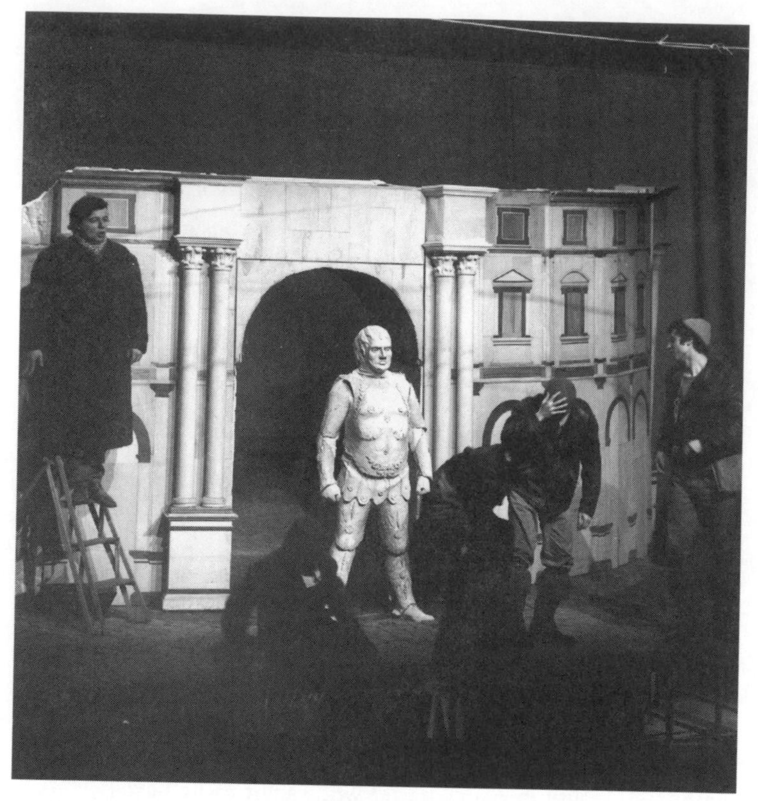

Plate 6 A scene from Chéreau's production. The mausoleum is still being built. Sganarelle (Marcel Maréchal) watches from a ladder.

logorrhoea and he falls down. In the fifth act, Sganarelle does not wait to be invited to speak, but explodes: 'Ah this time, that's more than I can stand, sir, I've got to say this, I can't stop myself...' Maréchal observed, and carefully marked in his performance, all the character's fumbling attempts to find his voice. Although Sganarelle never accedes to the language of his master and is left finally clamouring only for his wages, Maréchal saw a positive lesson in the story:

> The greatness of the character and the play is that they open up for Sganarelles of the future the royal highway to freedom: the mastery of language. Would you say that's a problem that no longer concerns us today?[73]

Like Pierrot who derives satisfaction from tricking a companion out of money, Sgaranelle constantly betrayed his failure to identify the interest of his class, for example by joining in the tormenting of the mendicant. But despite his lack of lucidity, and although at the end of the play he is left without a roof over his head or a day's wages, the production suggested that history is on his side. In a pre-production interview Chéreau stated that Sganarelle's alienation remained complete at the end of the play when 'he goes off to find another master. He has learned nothing, except perhaps that masters are not to be trusted, and progressive masters even less.'[74] However, in the performance itself a more millenary perspective was implied. Whatever Sganarelle felt as he witnessed his master being pulverised by the machine-statues, it was not sympathy. And there is the inescapable fact that at the end of the play Don Juan is dead but Sganarelle survives. In this respect he was like Brecht's soldier Schweik who is neither a collaborator nor a resister but who survives as an indestructible symbol of the people. The final image of Sganarelle was neither pathetic nor comic, but suggested rather a dawning of class awareness. The words 'My wages' were spoken first as a self-interrogation in a quiet tone. Turning to the workmen who were by now swarming over the Commander's tomb, he delivered his epilogue to them: 'Now he's dead, and everyone is satisfied...' With surprising brutality he pushed his master's body with his foot, then called again for his wages but this time shouting indignantly. The actor-stagehands who up to this point had watched the action with indifference, observed these events with manifest interest. Throwing away his hat, Sganarelle raised a clenched fist in the air and walked off – leaving the stagehands, now turned construction workers, to continue their task of building the future.

'DON JUAN' AT THE COMÉDIE-FRANÇAISE, 1952–1982

5 November 1952, Jean Meyer, director
4 February 1967, Antoine Bourseiller, director
26 May 1979, Jean-Luc Boutté, director
The 'Maison de Molière' had not performed *Don Juan* since the revival in 1925 of the 1917 staging. In all, barely a hundred performances had been presented there since the première, compared with nearly three thousand for *Tartuffe*. So in 1952, conscious of the significance of the event, it mustered all the considerable resources of a national theatre for the long-overdue new production. Directed by the company's most experienced Molière specialist, Jean Meyer, it assembled a distinguished cast with outstanding performers in the roles of Don Juan (Jean Debucourt), Sganarelle (Fernand Ledoux), and Elvire (Maria Casarès). The opening night was a gala performance with Charlie Chaplin's presence in the audience adding to the sense of a big occasion.

The predictable result was classical Molière in the somewhat dusty sense of the term. The director said he wanted to break with house traditions and to draw his inspiration from the text itself. This may seem an unexceptional statement but it had a special significance in the context of the Comédie-Française where 'tradition' meant an accretion of time-honoured ideas about roles, and handed-down bits of stage business to accompany them. Meyer did, in fact, re-think the staging, beginning by situating the action in its historical context: not in a conventional Sicilian landscape but in the French Court of Louis XIV. The setting, by the leading designer Suzanne Lalique, was noteworthy for the introduction of a theatricalist concept to the production (plate 7). It was a stylised *décor à transformations* inspired by seventeenth-century engravings of court stages involving theatre-within-theatre. The set consisted of a fixed perspective stage in the style of Louis XIV and, on another plane

Plate 7 Suzanne Lalique's stage setting for *Don Juan*, Comédie-Française, 1952.

further upstage, a sequence of backdrops depicting locations, with the scene changes taking place behind an upstage curtain. An impression of opulent grandeur in marble and gold in the architectural elements was combined with more delicate artistry in the backcloths. This conception was not unlike Golovin's design for Meyerhold's 1910 production in the way it incorporated a deliberate comment on the theatricality of the performance. The scenic design, however, did not seem to be reflected in any overall theatricalist conception of the play. And, after Christian Bérard's incomparable settings at the Athénée, it was felt by some to lack poetry. The same objection was made to the elaborate system of trapdoors and the spectacular final effects with fireworks.

Despite the renovation of the staging, however, the strictly conventional interpretation remained safely anchored in the Comédie-Française's traditional approach to the classical repertoire. Vilar, two years later, would argue that *Don Juan* was an expression of Molière's atheism. Meyer's premise, a more reassuring proposition for Comédie-Française subscribers, was that it was a fundamentally Christian play. He saw *Don Juan* as the riposte of an author who had been accused of impiety in *Tartuffe* and who wanted to demonstrate that he was not a free-thinker, making it the most Christian of Molière's works. So, he affirmed, 'Don Juan is Satan, the Statue is God, and Sganarelle is the ordinary man with his common sense and cowardice.'[75]

Just as Jouvet's production made it unavoidable that the Comédie-Française take up the challenge of *Don Juan*, so the latter's production no less inevitably invited comparison with the former. From this angle, Meyer's respectful approach was bound to disappoint, since Jouvet had led the public to expect something powerful, awesome. Probably the most disappointing aspect was the interpretation of the central character. Meyer's supposedly 'satanic' Don Juan was, in the event, not a conscious atheist, nor a free-thinker, nor an adversary of any divine force, but a shallow immoralist who takes pleasure in mocking society and convention. Jean Debucourt, adopting an off-hand manner and an ironic tone, presented an image of an elegant courtier and libertine whose cerebral delectation in vice prompted comparison with Valmont of *Les Liaisons dangereuses*. Although skilfully portrayed, the effect seemed lightweight. One critic called him 'a companiable cavalier'.[76] In the opinion of another, 'Don Juan is neither very dramatic nor very cynical, nor very caught up in the irresistible momentum of his passion. His discourse does not rise above the tone of drawing-room banter.'[77] Debucourt was a fine performer but, at fifty-eight, was no longer a young male lead. If the aim had been to present Don Juan as a character of substance the actor's maturity might have been a positive asset – Jouvet, for example, carried off a remarkable personal success in the role at the age of sixty. However, this was not the case here, and Debucourt (who had played Don Juan at the Odéon in 1922) was felt by many to be ten years too old. To another critic he suggested 'a Don Juan at the end of his amorous career'.[78]

Where the production suffered most in comparison with Jouvet's was in presenting Don Juan as a casual blasphemer, giving little sense that a matter of immense gravity was at stake. In the view of one critic:

> Debucourt is a great actor, one of our greatest, [but] he did not play Don Juan. He played only the Tartuffe-like aspect of Don Juan, feigning love for Charlotte and Mathurine, feigning virtue for Elvire and Carlos.[79]

However, an interpretation emphasing Don Juan as a charlatan (and thus highlighting a causal link with *Tartuffe*) did find favour with a number of veteran critics. Edmond See hailed it as the play's long-awaited resurrection,[80] while Dussane wrote:

> [Debucourt] made me see that for Molière Don Juan was, above all, a startling manifestation of the protean imposter-figure that haunted him. After Tartuffe the bourgeois imposter, Don Juan revealed the Court imposter.[81]

As a result, she professed, 'the text has never seemed more clearly illuminated'.[82]

Given Meyer's identification of the moral forces at work in the play, it followed that spectators were invited to sympathise wholeheartedly with Don Juan's victims. Don Louis (Jean Yonnel) was played like a father-figure from Cornelian tragedy: dignified like a Spanish grandee but not pompous, and allowing a noble sorrow to be glimpsed beneath his stoic exterior. There was not the least hint of any irony or ambivalence here, nor was there any in the presentation of the wronged wife. Played by Maria Casarès, the outstanding tragedienne of the period, Elvire was interpreted as a movingly sincere tragic heroine. An impression of the effect she made is given by the following: 'Casarès appears only in two scenes, but what scenes! The first, all contained indignation and sorrow. The second, all devastated resignation. One rarely sees anything in the theatre to compare with the way Casarès plays the first scene. One could scarcely imagine that so much passion could be combined with so much dignity.'[83] Robert Kemp found her 'truly passionate, Spanish, with that undertone of voluptuousness in her voice. And what beauty, without a trace of affectation or coquetry.'[84] Also remarked upon was the young Robert Hirsch who performed a much appreciated comic number in the role of Pierrot.

Apart from these highlights, the backbone of the production was Fernand Ledoux's Sganarelle. Ledoux succeeded in capturing the character's complexity while giving him a compelling human reality. His performance, built around the traditional framework of a servant with a strong instinct for self-preservation, embodied the naivety and cowardice traditionally associated with the role. But he also allowed himself a finely judged measure of cheeky irony in the face of his master, and moments of pathos which lifted the performance above conventionality. Critics were unanimous in their praise. 'He enters', wrote one, 'and suddenly the stage is animated, everything takes on substance and life. What humanity, what accurate observation, what wit!'[85] Another wrote: 'In his mouth the tirades become masterpieces of comic progression. And with a single line he can move the audience to tears. *Don Juan* is a must on account of Ledoux.'[86]

While restoring Sganarelle to the central place from which he had been displaced by Jouvet's overpowering Don Juan, the production did not strike the ideal balance between the two roles which Vilar's would achieve. Nevertheless, the performances found their target with the audiences who appreciated both the comic highlights and the scenes of pathos. Combining a reassuringly moral reading of the story with sumptuous classical staging, it was well attuned to the Comédie-Française's self-defined mission as curator of the classics. Progressive critics, however, were already becoming impatient with the timidity of that mission. One of them wrote, paradoxically, that the production was a betrayal of Molière: a betrayal not in the usual sense that the text was not respected, but because the servile respect for the text drained it of life.[87] In theatre, moderation can be a greater sin than excess.

The Meyer-Debucourt production was played in repertory for four months (a total of thirty-seven performances). Another fourteen years elapsed before the play was performed again, this time in an altogether bolder and more controversial version. By now (1967) the Comédie-Française was in the throes of crisis as the administration tried to come to terms with the movement for change, which in the theatre was already manifesting itself in a proliferation of new forms and modes of production. At the best of times the national theatre's ancient hierarchical structure of *sociétaires* and *doyens*, and its museum-like approach to the classics, can make it appear perennially outdated. But at times of profound social and cultural ferment, such as that which culminated in the events of May 1968, it comes under particular strain. The administration's response to the gathering crisis was to take measured steps to extend the repertoire and to make the company more receptive to modern directorial trends without sacrificing its traditional function or alienating conservatives within. In 1966 Ionesco (by then a modern classic) was admitted to the repertoire with a production of *Hunger and Thirst* by the independent director Jean-Marie Serreau. Such palliatives, annoying traditionalists while failing to satisfy progressivists, served only to deepen the sense of crisis.

Against this troubled background the administrator-general Maurice Escande (who had played Don Juan in 1922 and 1925) invited Antoine Bourseiller to mount a new production of *Don Juan.* It marked a considerably bolder move than the staging of Ionesco, partly because of Bourseiller's reputation as a young turk, and even more so because it opened the door to avant-garde experiment with the classical canon. It was not suprising in these circumstances that the new *Don Juan* became the Comédie-Française's most fiercely disputed production of the period.

Arriving at the Comédie-Française as a guest director, Bourseiller signalled his intentions with the provocative, albeit self-evident, statement that: 'Performing the classics in the way they were performed in 1665 is not tradition, it's laziness.'[88] This was coupled with the obligatory, though not necessarily insincere, assurances of respect for the play: 'At every stage I have referred constantly to Molière's text and followed it word for word.'[89] But, he added, 'without forgetting that we are in 1967... I'm in favour of tradition, as long as tradition means interpreting the classics, without betraying them, in the perspective of the present day.' The production did in fact adhere scrupulously to Molière's text with only two minor exceptions (Pierrot's description of Don Juan's clothes, which was omitted, and Sganarelle's pseudo-reasoning monologue, which became a dialogue with Don Juan). Bourseiller similarly denied that his intention was to impose any personal conception on the play: 'I just follow Molière. It's wrong for directors to distort plays with their own ideas. *Don Juan* is a masterpiece: there's nothing more to be said.'[90]

Despite its formal adherence to the text, the production offered a strikingly contemporary vision of the play. In a pre-première interview, Bourseiller explained that he saw Don Juan as

> a ghost journeying towards death. Neither Molière nor Tirso tells us where he comes from. He might be returning from a concentration camp. For me, the world of the concentration camp is present today, it's the source of our world. I have the impression that the atomic bomb originated there, that the atomic civilisation began there.[91]

Or again: 'Don Juan comes from nowhere, like a deportee from Buchenwald.'[92] Notwithstanding the apparent inanity of such remarks, the production captured perfectly the post-holocaust sensibility of the period, of which a metaphysical pessimism and the avoidance of a defined social context were major theatrical symptoms. From its absence of any historical referencing and the characteristic mood of eschatological angst, to the 1960s decorative style, it was an archetypal production of its time. Indeed, historians of style could well refer to it as a textbook illustration of the distinctive aesthetic of the period.

For the setting, Oskar Gustin designed a series of abstract metal sculptures and mobiles. In the first act these created a jagged, inhospitable landscape of beaten copper shapes, sharply angular or with curves coming to points. In the second act, located near a seashore, concave sheets of aluminium suggested stylised waves. For the forest in the third act, tall jagged shapes rose from the stage floor to meet suspended mobiles, all in polished brass. Angular welded metal shapes were similarly used to make chairs and a table for the fourth act (plate 8). The final act was played beneath a large copper sun with a ruby-coloured centre like a bloody eye. The effect overall was an uncomfortable, inhuman environment, which was accentuated by the mainly cold blue lighting. At the dramatic highpoints colour gels ranging from purple through to red contributed a nightmarish effect.

Gustin also created costumes which were intended to give a feel of timeless abstraction, though here too, with the passage of time, the 1960s look is very much in evidence. While Elvire, with long natural hair, wore a long velvet dress, the male characters wore close-fitting leather suits with distinctive collarless jackets like tunics, and leather boots. To some observers, doubtless influenced by the Apollo

Plate 8 Georges Descrières as Don Juan and Jacques Charon as Sganarelle (Comédie-Française, 1967).

space missions then taking place, the combined effect of sets and costumes suggested a lunar environment.

The settings prompted a lot of comment, much of it unfavourable. Some critics responded very angrily to what they saw as an act of provocation. *Le Figaro* wrote of Don Juan and Sganarelle wandering through 'an orgy of metallic monsters' and 'looking like motor-cyclists or a Wehrmacht tank crew'.[93] In the *New York Herald Tribune*, Wolfe Kaufman wrote wearily that it was 'just about the ugliest, most garish and most vulgar set that these tired old eyes have ever seen'.[94] But Guy Dumur, asserting the right of directors to create for their own time, wrote witheringly about fellow-critics who 'admit without any sense of shame that they have never set foot in a gallery of contemporary art'.[95] Bourseiller's own unanswerable response to criticisms was to say 'personally, I find cardboard sets and painted canvas ugly. And consequently, more provocative than copper.'[96]

The staging used the whole of the very considerable floor area, leaving wide tracts of space between the elements of decor. Bourseiller filled the space with a complex geometry of lateral and diagonal displacements, which the actors executed with long strides or in rushing movements. The result was to open the action up and to slow it down considerably. All this contributed to the sense of cosmic futility, though it had the effect, at times, of diluting the dramatic tension. The scene between Don Juan and his father was especially criticised in this respect. Bourseiller also employed a large number of 'extras' representing country folk or servants which gave the staging an almost operatic dimension. Another characteristic feature of the production was the extensive use of sound. The performance began with a crash of thunder, which was repeated periodically, and combined with the cry of seagulls, ringing bells and other less identifiable sounds ('a nightmare of noise' in the opinion of Kaufman). Amplified sound was widely employed in the 1960s by directors seeking to achieve environmental sensory effects. Like the use of the main characters as stagehands to change the scenery between acts, it was viewed by several critics as a gratuitous concession to current fashion. These reactions can be treated as irritability. An arguably more serious problem was that the somewhat grandiose staging tended to swamp the actors.

Don Juan was played by Georges Descrières in a sombre register. Bourseiller envisaged him as a free man in an absurd universe, who rejects all moral values and is fascinated by death. Descrières, a fine comic actor who had previously embodied a more conventional Don Juan in Robert Manuel's 1965 production, was an unusual choice. In the event, it was vindicated by Descrières' powerful performance as an angry nihilist. Some critics had reservations about the non-traditional conception of the role, a view expressed here by Jacques Carat: 'Descrières is a good Don Juan, unfortunately somewhat trapped in Bourseiller's conception of the role.'[97] However, the actor's skill in suggesting a tragic Don Juan was widely admired. According to one writer: '[his] performance reveals a great tragic actor: elegant, supple, he looks very beautiful and his technique is consummate perfection. He excels at expressing the character's weariness, suggesting a rather worn-out playboy.'[98]

Once again, though, it was Sganarelle who stole the show. Jacques Charon's Sganarelle was as far removed from the traditional idea of a comically naive valet as Descrières' Don Juan was from the image of the conventional seducer. Bourseiller integrated the role fully into the tragic perspective, making him a partner in Don Juan's experience of the absurd. All the traditional comic gags (the sneezes and pratfalls, and the business in the fourth act where Sganarelle steals food from his master's table) were eschewed. For some critics, this resulted in a loss of contrast. But Bourseiller's interpretation depended on the servant being seen as the master's partner in a human experience, rather than his social antithesis. This was well appreciated by Jacques Lemarchand, for whom the real revelation of the production was the complicity between Don Juan and Sganarelle:

> Jacques Charon has obviously grasped the importance of this rediscovered companion of Don Juan. He very sanely discards the traditions of the role. Of course, Sganarelle's clowning can be very reassuring to those who find Don Juan disturbing. The comic turns are relaxing. But in this production Sganarelle enters into the state of tension created by Don Juan, because he cannot live outside it. He is a participant in Don Juan's world, he becomes his friend – the only one, no doubt, that the friendless Don Juan can tolerate.[99]

Sganarelle thus emerged in this production as the last human contact of a man journeying towards death. Jacques Charon signalled from the first moments that he knew that Don Juan would go too far, and that he would stick by him: not as the timorous valet of the comic tradition, nor in the bourgeois tradition of the faithful servant, but, as one critic wrote, 'in a spirit of solidarity with a doomed companion on the edge of a precipice'.[100]

Obviously, this was not a performance to elicit easy laughter, but neither was it unrelievedly sombre. While shunning the obvious comic resources of the role, Charon substituted a more subtle comedy which underlined the tragedy. Jacques Carat wrote: 'He succeeds despite everything in bringing out a comedy in half-shades: the comedy of a fascinated impotence. His performance is marked by admirable finesse and humanity.'[101] The few dissenting voices again attributed the blame to Bourseiller's conception of the play. According to one: 'Jacques Charon, prevented from playing Molière's Sganarelle and unable or unwilling to play the one imposed by Bourseiller, compounds the director's misunderstanding by contributing a bastard performance.'[102] In contrast, Guy Dumur wrote that the production showed Charon as 'a great actor who is finally revealed in his true light by Bourseiller'.[103]

In the absurd universe created by the play, the secondary characters also ceased to be defined as social types and emerged in a mainly sympathetic light. One of the production's revelations was the very positive depiction of Pierrot, played by Jean-Pierre Roussillon with 'stunning dignity, tenderness and anger'.[104] The scene with Don Juan's creditor was similarly seen in a new light as an integral part of a serious drama instead of a comic interlude. Michel Aumont imbued a sense of dignity to M. Dimanche, making him not the butt of Don Juan's tomfoolery but a tragic victim of his desperate rage, which went as far as subjecting him to physical torture. Also unusual – but less successfully so – was Ludmila Mikael's Elvire. A young graduate of the Conservatoire appearing in her first professional role, Mikael lacked the authority to impose Elvire's character.

This miscasting was one of several errors of judgement that marred the production. (Another was the director's idea of having her perform a strip-tease to seduce Don Juan in their first scene together, a miscalculation which was corrected after the preview performances).

Overall, the production offers a classic illustration of the strengths and weaknesses of a directorial style which emphasises impressionistic climate at the expense of cogent analysis. Visceral rather than cerebral, it created a coherent self-contained stage universe. Its disturbing, neurotic qualities account for the powerful experience of the play that many critics reported. But spectators who wished to organise this experience in terms of a coherent analysis would have found it a difficult task. One reason for this was the shift into intemporality and abstraction which robbed the characters of their social motivation. In Bourseiller's interpretation, Don Juan's free-thinking, which can only be explicable in the context of a certain social milieu, was transformed into a more diffuse nihilism, and the sense of a character in revolt was replaced by a baroque exultation in his own tragic destiny.

The production also highlights the problem posed by the supernatural in a secular world. As one critic observed at the time, 'The scene with the Beggar and the scenes with the Statue have lost their point because they are meaningless to a purely modern mind.'[105] It would be more accurate to say that they need to be given a *different* meaning. In *Don Juan*, where the supernatural plays both a thematic and a dramatic role, several strategies are available to modern directors. In some productions, such as those of Vilar and Bergman, it becomes a theatrical artifice which is not intended to command belief. In others, such as those of Chéreau, Planchon and Sobel, it acquires ideological significance as the theatrical expression of a social force. A more radical option, adopted by Grossman, is to eliminate it altogether. Bourseiller's production, while situating the play in a de-christianised world, seemed not to have resolved this central question. If the Statue, impressively represented by a skeleton seen beneath a fleshy form, could be construed as a purely secular representation of death, the constant rumble of thunder that punctuated the performance suggested some obscure divine anger. According to one commentator, 'from the very first moment, with the first crash of thunder, the supernatural speaks', making the play 'a tragedy, in which the principal character is God who controls every step from behind metal screens'.[106] But, as the same critic pointed out, if everything is settled in advance, not only are the intercessions of Elvire and Don Louis superfluous, but also Don Juan's assertions of atheism are nullified by the dramatic action. Little wonder that Gary O'Connor, writing for the *Financial Times*, confessed: 'I remain unsure about what M. Bourseiller was trying to say.'[107]

Beyond the intrinsic interest of Bourseiller's interpretation, this production was also significant in reviving the perennial debate about the rights and responsibilities of directors in relation to classical texts. Traditionalists clinging to the notion of a universal essence embodied in a sacrosanct text were enraged by it. Christian Megret concluded his objections to the production thus: 'In any case, even if modernising *Don Juan* were not a fundamentally stupid enterprise, respect for the text should have prevented it. Antoine Bourseiller has no right to tamper with Molière.'[108] Countering such objections were those like Guy Dumur, who asserted the right of each generation to re-interpret the classics anew and reminded fellow critics 'that the repertoire is not a museum, and that every age should present its own vision of a masterpiece'.[109] Also at issue, of course, was the role of France's first national theatre. What made the experiment especially intolerable, for Megret, was the fact that it was permitted to happen in the Comédie-Française: 'How can the administration of the Maison de Molière have allowed it? Ah, what's to be done when firemen catch fire?'[110] Against this curious image of a national theatre entrusted with the mission of extinguishing innovation, Dumur proposed the exact converse: 'Whatever one thinks of the production – and it certainly does call for discussion – one cannot underestimate the importance it assumes in the context of the

Comédie-Française which has sunk into a state of lethargy and a dearth of creativity that are unworthy of a great theatre.'[111]

Given what was at stake, one may regret that the production itself was not more resoundingly convincing, for Dumur was self-evidently correct to welcome the initiative. One recalls Charles Dullin's pleasure at the decision of the young iconoclast Barrault to join a stagnating Comédie-Française in 1939. The move horrified many of Barrault's friends, but in the opinion of his Cartel mentor it was 'carrying the struggle into the citadel itself'.[112] It is in this perspective, perhaps, that Bourseiller's experiment should be appreciated.

Storming the citadel, however, like re-inventing the classics, is something that each generation has to undertake anew. Twelve years later, in 1979, the Comédie-Française was again plunged into controversy when it sought to re-interpret *Don Juan* in an up-to-date *mise en scène*. A flavour of the reaction which greeted Jean-Luc Boutté's production is conveyed by the following:

> *Don Juan* at the Comédie-Française, directed and designed by Jean-Luc Boutté, has qualities that take one's breath away... Boutté has cleared the ground, opened the play up and allowed it to breath, and Molière's text has an almost tangible clarity. With its transparency restored, *Don Juan* retains all its scandalous power.[113]

> One is dazzled, at times, by its veritable greatness. In a setting that recalls Jouvet's *L'Illusion comique*, Jean-Luc Boutté gives us an original spectacle, poetic, intelligent and superbly rhythmed.[114]

Alternatively:

> A more pretentiously stupid *mise en scène* has rarely been seen at the Comédie-Française. It is enough to make one very angry: *Don Juan* assassinated, debased, obliterated by people who seem to be illiterates.[115]

> So this is the *Don Juan* created to mark the three hundredth anniversary of the Comédie-Française, alias the 'Maison de Molière'.

> We have to resign ourselves to the fact, but we should not accept it. For it is hard to imagine a more insipid, futile performance, a production more replete with misinterpretation in virtually every line, than this *Don Juan*.[116]

This time, however, the critical divide was not a straightforward split between traditionalists and progressives. Certainly, there were the familiar proprietorial voices protesting about liberties taken with a classical text. However, on this occasion they were joined by critics whom one would not tax with conservatism but who found the production insipid and derivative.

In truth, Boutté's *Don Juan*, the third production of a brilliant young *sociétaire*, was hardly a revolutionary event, though it introduced techniques of historical deconstruction to offer a multilayered reading of the text and the legend. Such an approach, although innovatory in the context of the Comédie-Française's more conventional house style, had become familiar enough to theatregoers through the work of directors such as Planchon. Boutté himself trained under Planchon and Maréchal in Lyon before studying at the Conservatoire prior to entering the Comédie-Française in 1971, but it would be misleading to describe him as a disciple of Planchon. He is suspicious of the creative powers assumed by directors in modern theatre and claims no didactic intentions for his productions. His productions certainly display none of Planchon's ideological commitment, though their style does perhaps owe something to the latter's concept of directing as 'scenic writing'.

Performed in a setting of refined beauty evoking a collapsing civilisation, *Don Juan* depicted a *fin de siècle* soul-sickness. Once again, Molière's image of a 'wicked nobleman' was replaced by an image of a man consumed by an existential sense of futility. The central character here personnified not *le mal* but *le mal de vivre*, since Don Juan was a man who has seen through the hollowness of religion and morality, but for whom rationalist materialism does not provide sufficient justification for continuing to live. To this extent the interpretation had a distant similarity to Bourseiller's, but instead of the strident climate that marked the latter's, this production was performed in a subdued, elegiac tone. The play was a suicidal cry but, Boutté insisted, 'Don Juan utters his cry without anger or bitterness. It's a cry of generosity, the cry of an artist, a creator who refuses the logic of two plus two.'[117]

Few productions of the play can have offered a more indulgent portrait of the central character. Boutté had said in an interview that he was struck by the poignancy of Don Juan's fate. Observing that he is the only character in Molière's theatre who is killed, he went on to say:

> More than any other play by Molière, this one speaks to us, to our humanity. It depicts a man's life. By chance, or by an act of will, this life leads Don Juan to death. And this death is intolerable, for the death of a young man, even if he is smiling, is inescapably tragic. Especially when he has everything: beauty, wealth, nobility.[118]

In another interesting observation, he stated that Don Juan is 'the most generous character in all Molière's theatre'.[119] Whereas many directors see either cynicism or self-deception behind Don Juan's claim to an aristocratic generosity of spirit (i.e. an abuse of '*noblesse oblige*'), Boutté saw him as a character devoid of calculation or self-interest. The gift of money to the Beggar, for example, was given spontaneously. Similarly, in the first encounter with Elvire's brother, he offered himself voluntarily up to Don Alonso's sword in a gesture that was plainly sincere. Francis Huster, the actor who created the role in 1979, confirmed this conception of the character when he told reporters: 'I will not be an arrogant, self-confident Don Juan. No virtuoso numbers. I play him sincerely. He is not a hypocrite or a liar.'[120]

An interesting consequence of this approach, dramatically, was to diminish the usual sense of conflict between Don Juan and the other characters, whom he saw less as antagonists than as mirrors of his inner self. The interaction between characters thus became a process of revelation rather than a struggle for domination. José-Maria Flotats, who replaced Huster in a later revival, enlarged on this aspect of the role. Don Juan, he said,

> is a poet, like Rimbaud, one who not merely surprises but who shocks and scandalises, a provocative presence and a creator; and that is what makes him a liberating presence. He does not break the people that he meets along the way. They constitute a series of tests, they modify him, but also he modifies them.[121]

It was a markedly youthful production. In contrast to the middle-aged Don Juans of Jouvet, Vilar and Debucourt, the tendency of directors since the 1970s to demythologise the legend has led to Don Juan being envisaged as a younger and often less weighty character. Boutté's production followed this tendency, even to the point of making Don Juan appear fragile. Francis Huster played him as a self-admiring young nobleman who viewed society with a detached irony (plate 9). His languid attitude seemed at times to denote a terminal weariness. Only the hint of a fixed smile permanently playing around his mouth, accentuated by the fine line of a thin moustache, suggested the implacable character of someone devoid of self-pity. Huster went for none of the powerful dramatic effects aimed at by Jouvet or Vilar, but within its limited dramatic range it was an intelligent and finely etched performance, producing an impression that was both fascinating and irritating. As Nicholas Powell wrote, Huster's Don Juan was 'subtle, archly self-conscious and sensual to the point of effeminacy. He is simultaneously sympathetic and repulsive.'[122]

Boutté shaped the dramatic action on the motif of a journey. Don Juan's episodic itinerary through the Sicilian landscape with his companion Sganarelle became the metaphorical figuration of a journey towards death:

> Is Don Juan's journey a suicidal decline? I do not think it is possible to give an unequivocal answer to this question. I opted merely to represent Don Juan's evolution as that of a man casting off all his attributes, all the codes of the time, until he is finally left naked, alone and himself, standing face to face with death.[123]

Plate 9 Francis Huster as Don Juan and Patrice Kerbrat as Sganarelle (Comédie-Française, 1979).

Hence the transformation which Don Juan's costumes underwent during the course of the evening. Initially he was seen wearing the costume of a fashion-conscious aristocrat of 1665 including a profusion of silk ribbons, a plumed hat and a voluminous frizzy blond wig. It was reproduced with historical precision, as were all the costumes, but their theatricality was heightened by an idealised range of soft colours, mainly saffron, pink and pastel blue. Don Juan's progressive detachment from life was represented by the discarding of his court costume, beginning after the boating incident in the second act and then in his disguise as a pilgrim in the third act. In the fourth act he was seen with a shawl wrapped around an undershirt and the court wig of the first act was replaced by a lank black domestic wig (plate 10). For his final appointment with death, he appeared bare-headed and wearing only a white cotton undershirt like an enveloping chasuble.

While the hero underwent this metamorphosis, a parallel but inverse transformation affected the decor. Conceived by Boutté with his assistant designer Philippe Kerbrat, it was set upon a wide, open stage backed by a sky-cloth producing a powerful impression of space and luminosity. What spectators saw at first, occupying almost the entire stage area, was an orangey-brown platform like an island set in the deep blue sea of the stage floor itself. Examining it, one could see that its contours depicted a stylised map-line outline of Sicily. The reference to Sicily is one which many directors choose to disregard – with some justification since Molière's version, despite the staging note that 'the scene is in Sicily', was a thoroughly gallicised *Don Juan* in its ideas and social environment. For Boutté, however, the Sicilian location was one of the traces left on the play by the circumstances in which it was written because, he argued, the geographical displacement of the action was a necessary ploy to which Molière was forced to resort when treating a subject as audacious as atheism.[124]

As well as hinting at Molière's struggles with the devout set, the setting had a complex symbolic function. A central feature of the concept was the visible presence of the cosmic elements, which Boutté spoke of in these terms:

> On the one hand I wanted to reproduce Sicily according to contemporary drawings of 1665. On the other hand I wanted the four elements of the universe that constitute the context for Don Juan's journey to be present from the opening scene. The sea and the sky are represented by dark blue stage cloths; fire is represented by the sun, but it also mingles with the earth of this island set in the sea; the earth is not only parched by the sun, it also resembles solidified lava, since Sicily is volcanic: it's a combination of earth and fire.[125]

Plate 10 A scene from Act IV of Boutté's production. Patrice Kerbrat (Sganarelle), Jacques Toja (Don Louis) and Francis Huster (Don Juan).

Into this metaphorical landscape fragments of scenic accessories were introduced, representing a disorderly bric-à-brac of cultural debris (plate 10). In the first act there were just two wooden caryatids in the form of angels, bleached white as if washed up by the sea. Subsequently, fragments of colonnade, candelabra, a retable and other devotional objects appeared. The principle was one of selective realism whereby real objects placed in an overtly theatrical setting lose their naturalistic qualities and become charged with symbolic significance. While insisting on their emblematic function, Boutté declined to attribute precise values to the scenic accessories, preferring to stress their ambivalence:

> The debris of a cataclysm? of a volcanic eruption? of an act of vandalism? Perhaps the vestiges of a revolt by Don Juan (or somebody else?) against the Commander, or against the religion of men who worship God through the cult of icons? According to the way the stage is lit and the way the objects are laid out or heaped up, the stage represents Don Juan's home, a sea-shore, a forest, a derelict cemetery. My scenery is deliberately ambiguous; progressively, it resembles a gilded 'discharge'; in a way, it represents the destruction of a devotional cult: the fact that men build statues, tabernacles and tombs, does not make God exist.[126]

There was a complex symbolism, too, in the use of theatrical time. The performance represented one day as traced by the passage of the sun: sunrise, zenith, sunset, providing a simple but suggestive theatrical metaphor for the duration of a life. The opening scene began just before daybreak, and in the second scene the cyclorama brightened to represent a golden dawn at the moment when Don Juan first appeared in his resplendent costume. As the day advanced, and the clear blue sky turned to a white midday heat (Act II), little stylised clouds started to appear in the sky. In the third act, the light was more livid and the clouds gathered into a heavier mass. Eventually the sun became completely obscured and darkness fell. In parallel to this, a stylised vegetation was springing up: innocent pastoral vines and brambles in the second act, a heavier covering of vegetation for the forest in the third act, and by the fifth act ivy and moss engulfing the disordered ruins.

In these ways, Boutté used stage lighting and scenic accessories to create two overlapping time scales: a narrative time (the duration of Don Juan's journey) in which the action was represented, and another more metaphorical time in which a parallel commentary was constructed. The performance as a whole thus described a double movement of entropy: on the one hand, the progressive denuding of Don Juan as he approached his own death; and on the other hand the more invasive but increasingly chaotic accumulation of signs evoking Christian civilisation falling into decay.

In addition to representing the collapse of faith as seen from a modern vantage point the production hinted at the specific context of Molière's (and Louis XIV's) struggle with the Compagnie du Saint-Sacrement. The progressive masking of the sun could be read as an allusion to the way in which Molière's protector, the self-styled Sun King, abandoned the theatrical pleasures of his youth as the devout set acquired a stronger hold over him in the later years of his reign. The back-stage machinations of the *dévots* were also suggested in the sinister transformation of Elvire between her first and second appearances. In the first act one saw a lover motivated by a sincere and tender passion. Her costume (riding dress and boots) suggested a woman of energy and determination. When Elvire reappears in the fourth act she speaks not directly of love but of repentance. Jouvet always considered her renunciation of Don Juan to be one of the most tragically beautiful expressions of love anywhere in the theatre. Boutté gave it a very different interpretation. On her second appearance she was dressed in penitent's robes. Her earlier independent spirit was broken, her gestures mechanical, and she gave the impression that she was reciting pious words learnt by heart. In this way, Boutté said, Elvire betrays how 'she has been recuperated by the *dévots* who are manipulating her now'.[127]

While recognising that one of the play's given elements is a miraculous event which cannot be reduced to a wholly rational explanation, the production played down its supernatural significance. As for the Statue, in one sense it was assimilated to the other broken and useless devotional artefacts that littered the stage. In another sense, Boutté incorporated it into Don Juan's personal destiny, while endowing it with a certain element of mystery and ambiguity. All one saw of the Commander's statue, in fact, was a truncated Roman-style bust which was seen resting at a tilting angle on the stage floor, as if the upper part of some once whole statue adorning a mausoleum had fallen to the ground. On the bust was the head of a Sicilian puppet which, when invited to supper, nodded and then fell off. As Boutté said, 'in the context of, say, a possible earth tremor, it could just as easily have been a falling column.' But, he added, 'that still does not rule out the possibility that the falling head is a supernatural sign'.[128] In Act IV, where Sganarelle signals a terrifying apparition at the door, Don Juan exited from the stage and returned carrying the puppet's head. Again, said Boutté, spectators were free to read into this a metaphysical sign or to opt for a rational explanation:

> It can be comic, it can be fantastical: the puppet's head may represent a skull, the symbol of man's capacity for reflection upon the meaning of existence; it could equally be a final warning from the *dévots* or Elvire's brothers who may have placed it outside his door.[129]

It was Don Juan himself, in a pensive voice like Hamlet addressing Yorick's skull, who spoke the Commander's words inviting him to supper. The dénouement itself conveyed no sense of divine wrath, and no descent into hell. At the scene of the Commander's tomb, the puppet-head was restored to its original place on the bust. In response to an unseen voice, Don Juan proferred his hand to an invisible presence and collapsed slowly as the life drained out of him. Ultimately, this seemed to suggest, the Commander was a manifestation not of some divine power but of the inner mystery which leads Don Juan to choose death.

Like Bourseiller, Boutté played down the social distinction between Don Juan and Sganarelle, treating the latter as a companion rather than a servant. Patrice Kerbrat as Sganarelle said: 'Francis [Huster] and I try to establish a relationship between equals. It creates room for freedom of expression and tenderness. Don Juan plays for the benefit of Sganarelle.'[130] The result was an unusually self-confident Sganarelle, to the bemusement of critics like Powell who noted that 'Francis Huster is set off by a boisterous and sympathetic Sganarelle who argues surprisingly democratically with his master. More whining and cringing on his part would better have set off the cruelty of his position.'[131] In fact, a different relationship was established when Huster was replaced by José-Maria Flotats for the revival in 1982. Flotats stayed within Boutté's original conception of the role, as his description of it reveals: 'Don Juan is a personification of the inability to live with oneself, he is the spirit of revolt made man, the non-acceptance of self, of the human condition.'[132] However, the actor's very different personality produced a more emphatic, energetic Don Juan. Flotats' performance is evoked here by Dominique Jamet:

> Frightening yet seductive, attractive and repulsive, putting as much urgent passion into persuading a peasant he is going to marry her merely to steal a kiss, as he does into persuading Elvire to spend the night with him, what this voluptuous Don Juan loses in the spiritual dimension he gains in carnal force. Since Jouvet I have never seen an actor possess the entire role. At least Flotats' Don Juan lacks neither power nor coherence.[133]

In 1979 Huster's Don Juan was dominated by Kerbrat's Sganarelle both in physique and presence. With Flotats this was no longer the case, with the result that traces of the familiar *ancien régime* relationship of master to servant started to reappear.

Boutté's *Don Juan*, the most recent to date by the Comédie-Française, was certainly the company's most polished production of the play. Some critics responded positively to what Jean-Jacques

Gautier saw as a 'visual richness combined with sobriety of expression' where 'the preoccupation with form masks a painful inner tension'.[134] 'Don't miss it at any cost', wrote another, 'for the great story of spirit and matter is here complete. Everything is made blindingly clear in the twilight shadows.'[135] But, as already indicated, it drew some angry responses. Hostile critics were uncertain which was worse: the central character or Boutté's design. Of the former, it was said that 'Huster's Don Juan is nothing: a literal nullity, pure absence; neither eroticism, nor atheism, there is nothing left but a self-satisfied kitten.'[136] As for the decor, it was likened to 'a Faubourg St Honoré shop window: cheap baroque out of a bazaar or coffee-table magazine. And the costumes are stupid … all chocolate-box colours, vaguely gilded: a sickly confection.'[137]

My own reservations were of a different order. As an aesthetic experiment it was a staging of great formal elegance and impeccably executed. By means of simple but meticulous accessories and lighting, coupled with sumptuous costuming, Boutté created an effect which was strangely beautiful and suffused thoughout with an end-of-epoch sense of decline. The danger arises when the aestheticising impulse extends to the central character himself. There was undeniable poignancy in Huster's indulgent presentation of Don Juan as a *poète maudit.* The result was a quietly elegiac *Don Juan* – but bloodless. The question really is whether one wants stronger meat. Or, as a critic asked: 'Is this the scandalous play that angered the *dévots* so much that Molière was forced to withdraw it?'[138]

CHAPTER 3

MAJOR PRODUCTIONS ON THE MODERN EUROPEAN STAGE

A MODERNIST 'DON JUAN' IN ST PETERSBURG (VSEVOLOD MEYERHOLD, DIRECTOR)

Alexandrinsky Theatre, 9 November 1910

I entered the hall of the Alexandrinsky Theatre well before the start of the performance and stopped, astonished by the sight in front of me. There is no curtain on the stage. The oval of red velvet boxes in the auditorium is joined to the stage in harmonious ensemble with a huge false proscenium. My rapt gaze is lost in the splendour of the wings, screens, lambrequins, and the tapestry curtain in the background which for the moment conceals the wonders of Golovin's pictures ... Above the forestage hang three large chandeliers with wax candles, their wicks connected by threads. At each side of the forestage there are large candelabra on pedestals. The boxes and stalls are full of well-dressed spectators. You can hear a buzz and a whisper of admiration. Something is about to happen ...

Two blackamoors come out of the wings from opposite sides. They are the proscenium servants and they carry long sticks with lighted tapers. They set fire to the threads on the chandeliers. The fire starts to run through the threads and ignites all the candles on the chandeliers and candelabra. The living flames gives off the vibrating light which no electricity can produce.

When the tapestry curtain upstage is drawn back, one beholds not a decorative backdrop but, in a golden picture-frame, a magnificent canvas by Golovin which will be changed for every scene.

Having set the stage, the blackamoors ring handbells, whereupon

> two prompters dressed in costumes and wigs, carrying texts of the play in bound portfolios, emerge from the wings and sit down behind special screens, their heads plainly visible through cut-outs, and the performance begins.
>
> The blackamoors carry in a golden armchair and set it down on the proscenium, and then the monumental figure of Sganarelle-Varlamov appears from the depth of the stage. He is the public's favourite. In a storm of applause he comes down to the proscenium, into the fully-lit auditorium, settles himself in the armchair, and takes a goodly amount of snuff in his nostrils. He sneezes, smiles, looks amiably about the public in the boxes and stalls. He feels himself very comfortable. Sganarelle gazes upon the spectators' faces, entering into a real and trusting relation with them. I caught his eye on me twice. The fatal line separating the stage from the auditorium is obliterated.[1]

So begins the description by one of Meyerhold's students of a legendary first night which two decades later a historian of the Alexandrinsky Theatre was to call 'one of the most overwhelming events in the history of the European theatre'.[2] Bebutov's account emphasises the novelty of Meyerhold's treatment of decorative elements of staging, the anti-illusionist presentation, and the special relationship that was created between stage and auditorium. In this way it signals that for Meyerhold's contemporaries the production's significance lay less in the interpretation of a specific play than in the revelation of a new theatrical aesthetic. A showcase for all Meyerhold's ideas at the time, it was seen as inaugurating a revolutionary theatricalist approach to the classics and became a landmark in Russian modernism.

Meyerhold was the first all-powerful director of the Russian stage. Against the changing background of Russian theatre from the 1890s to the 1930s, through naturalism, symbolism, modernism, constructivism and post-revolutionary socialist realism, none of which he fully embraced, he pursued a personal brand of stylised theatricalism. In 1898 he was a founder member of the Moscow Art

Theatre where Stanislavsky was exploring his revolutionary style of acting aimed at creating a complete illusion of reality. But Meyerhold was never at home within the confines of naturalism and soon developed a deep and lasting dislike both for illusionist staging and for Stanislavsky's concentration on the idea of character, with its emphasis on psychological realism. That, and his growing belief in the need to subordinate the actor and all aspects of production to the absolute control of the director soon brought him into conflict with the Art Theatre's director. Following a violent quarrel with Stanislavsky in 1902, he aligned himself with the wave of anti-naturalist experiment that was sweeping Europe. After a period experimenting with stylised productions of the new symbolist drama, he joined Vera Komissarzhevskaya's company in St Petersburg as its artistic director (1906–7). Here his experiments with impressionistic stylisation drew hostile responses from the critical establishment which treated him as faddish, extravagant and a charlatan, and alarmed even Komissarzhevskaya. But Meyerhold was already moving on. Having rejected realism, and after being the first to introduce symbolist drama to Russia, he became impatient with the occultist tendencies of symbolism and its separation from real life. At a time of increasing social and political ferment, he wanted 'to burn with the spirit of the times'[3] and was already looking for a form of theatre which would engage with actuality. In 1907 Komissarzhevskaya expelled him from her theatre, but by now Meyerhold had already concluded, as he later wrote, that 'The way of Mystery and the way of Theatre do not merge.'[4] The main outline of his theatrical project had already taken shape: a theatre which was neither naturalist not symbolist but stylised and self-consciously theatrical, radical in content, and drawing on the techniques of popular tradition to create more direct relationships with the audience.

It was at this time that V. Telyakovsky, Director of the Imperial Theatres in St Petersburg, invited him to take over the artistic direction of the Alexandrinsky Theatre and its associated opera house the Mariinksy. It was a bold move by Telyakovsky, who noted in his diary: 'Meyerhold has frequently been attacked by the public and in the press, and this strong hostility towards him has convinced me that he must be interesting in some way.'[5] The invitation caused a sensation, and outright hostility in some quarters, especially among members of the company. To allay their fears, Telyakovsky let it be known that Meyerhold had 'retreated substantially from his initial excess and understands his errors in Komissarzhevskaya's theatre'.[6] Moreover, it was understood that 'there can be no excesses on the model stage', nor was there any question of 'transforming the Alexandrinsky into a stylised theatre'. It was also agreed that the repertoire would give special place to the Russian and European classics rather than the modernist works with which Meyerhold had recently been experimenting. In short, claimed Telyakovsky, there was even a danger he might turn into a conformist in his new surroundings.[7] In this way the most formidable iconoclast of the Russian theatre was put in charge of one of the country's most conservative institutions. Far from succumbing to tradition, he set about making it one of the most innovative stages in Russia.

Meyerhold had been sincere when he told Telyakovsky his current interest lay with the classics. For some time his experiments had led him to reflect on what contribution performance styles of earlier ages could make to the renewal of modern theatre, and he had thought greatly about the question of how works of the past should be presented and made relevant to present-day audiences. According to Meyerhold, some plays from the past are so steeped in the moment of their original creation that they 'cannot be appreciated unless they are presented in a form which attempts to create for the modern spectator conditions identical to those which the spectator of the past enjoyed'.[8] In Meyerhold's mind this did not mean slavishly reproducing the material details. Rather, it meant seeking the secret of the play's meaning in the architectural form of the theatre of its time and in the spirit of the historical moment at which it was created. His production of *Don Juan* was just such an experiment in 'scenic reconstructivism'.

First, the architectural form: referring to recent experiments at Evreinov's Ancient Theatre involving 'authentic' reconstructions of ancient performance traditions, he wrote that:

> in producing a work from a past age of theatre it is by no means obligatory to stage it *according to the archaeological method*; in the process of reconstruction there is no need for the director to bother with exact re-creation of the architectural characteristics of the stage of the period in question.[9]

In order to stage Molière's *Don Juan*, he went on, it would be futile to try to create a literal replica of the playwright's Palais-Royal theatre. The principle to be applied was rather that of 'a *free composition* in the spirit of the theatre in which it was originally staged'. But, he added, on one condition: that 'from the old theatre one must select those architectural features which best convey the spirit of the work'. Meyerhold had no doubt about which architectural feature expressed the spirit of Molière's comedy: it was the proscenium or forestage, the point of contact between the actors and the audience. Believing that the audience had a creative role to play in theatre, in his search for a more participatory form of drama Meyerhold's attention had become increasingly focused on the question of the forestage. At the same time he was exploring a theory of acting which would increase the spectators' involvement in the theatrical event. This was one of the fundamental differences he had with Stanislavsky. In naturalist theatre, the illusion of reality is sustained by the actors remaining scrupulously oblivious to the spectators' presence. The performer's attention is concentrated exclusively on the events on stage, assigning a voyeuristic role to the audience who observe the illusion as through a transparent fourth wall. In Meyerhold's view this exclusion of the spectator was a denial of the true function of drama, since it is in the inter-action between actor and audience that the theatrical event in forged. Thus Meyerhold's notion of the actor was opposed to Stanislavsky's on every key issue: he must be a virtuoso instrument at the service of the director (technique, not intuitive identification, is what counts); he must lack individuality (only by depersonalising himself can he convey accurately the director's conception); and instead of focusing his creative effort inwards, towards his 'character', the ideal actor 'stands *face to face with the spectator*, thus intensifying the fundamental relationship of performer and spectator'.[10]

All these ideas on staging and acting came together in the production of *Don Juan* whose overriding aim was to make modern spectators experience the dramatic and satirical force of the play in the way it was felt by seventeenth-century audiences. The stage design and scenic decoration, and the actors themselves, were all employed as instruments to lead the spectators to a critical understanding of the play.

Where the theatrical form was concerned, Meyerhold stated that Molière's comic art was straining against the limitations of the stage of his time:

> If we go to the heart of Molière's works, we find that he was trying to remove the footlights from the contemporary stage, since they were better suited to the heroic drama of Corneille than to plays with their origins in the popular theatre. The academic theatre of the Renaissance failed to take advantage of the projecting forestage, keeping actor and audience at a mutually respectful distance... How could Molière accept this segregation of actor and public?[11]

Historically, it is incorrect to say that Molière performed his plays on a proscenium stage or that he removed the footlights. Meyerhold's meaning, I think, is that whilst Molière worked on an Italianate perspective stage, framed by the proscenium arch, the roots and spirit of his art lay in popular performance traditions characterised by physical proximity and a presentational style of acting. This was why, Meyerhold said, Molière's drama was trying to burst out of the architectural constraints of the seventeenth-century stage. Hemmed in behind the footlights, 'how could his exuberant humour have its proper effect under such conditions? How could the whole range of his bold, undisguisedly authentic characterization be accommodated within such a space? How could the waves of accusatory monologue of an author outraged by the banning of *Tartuffe* reach the spectator from such a distance?'[12]

The production's designer was Alexander Golovin, the outstanding stage artist of the period. In 1909 Meyerhold sent Golovin a first note about *Don Juan*, prescribing a stage divided into two planes:

> 1. The proscenium, constructed according to architectural principles, intended exclusively for 'reliefs' and the figures of the actors (who perform only on this area). The proscenium to have a forestage projecting deep into the auditorium. No footlights. No prompt box.
>
> 2. The upstage area, intended exclusively for painted backdrops, is not used by the actors at all, except in the finale (downfall and immolation of Juan), and even then they will appear only on the dividing line between the two areas.[13]

As Konstantin Rudnitsky writes, 'in these few words a programme of blinding innovation and astounding boldness was set forth'.[14] Two distinct planes, one pictorial, the other dynamic, were combined within a unified overall concept. Footlights, prompt box and orchestra pit disappeared. A large semi-circular forestage where all the action was to take place was built out deep into the auditorium, covering the orchestra pit and reaching to the front row of the stalls. The design of the Empire-style auditorium was carried through on to a false proscenium arch, linking the auditorium and boxes to the stage in such a way that the performance space seemed to be within the auditorium. The stage was decorated in red and gold, matching the auditorium, and the stage floor was covered by a pale blue carpet. Furniture and props, which were brought on and removed by stage assistants, were reduced to a bare minimum: a row of armchairs facing the audience in Act I, some trees centre-stage in Act III, and a table and chairs for Act IV.

On the upstage plane, behind the proscenium arch, was a shallow stage where the painted scenes would be displayed, framed by russet-and-gold decorated drapes and festoons. For these scenes Golovin designed a series of impressionistic paintings which were art works in their own right. The first act ('a palace') was treated as an interior-exterior – hence the candelabra and chairs on stage and the backcloth with a view of an idealised landscape with passing carriage (plate 11). Act II depicted a stylised 'Sicilian' village (in reality it looked rather Spanish) with white-walled houses and cliffs rising against a pale blue sky. The third act represented a wood in fading evening light. Towards the end of the act the light faded completely and the painted cloth was removed to reveal the sepulchre and Statue bathed in phosphorescence. In Act IV (Don Juan's apartment) the backcloth showed a pair of tall French windows, framed in an ornate casement. The backcloth itself was pierced by pinholes through which light shone like stars against a deep blue background. The final act showed a painted pastoral landscape supplemented by a painted screen.

All the scene changes took place behind a tapestry curtain, which was drawn closed by actors in full view of the audience and opened again in an overtly theatrical gesture, to reveal each new scene. Since the upstage area was intended only for pictorial effects, the actors never crossed the proscenium line except at the very beginning, when Sganarelle made his first appearance from upstage, and the very end, when Don Juan took the Statue's hand and was led down through a trapdoor to hell. By starting and finishing the play with this 'framing' device, Meyerhold emphasised that the characters' only existence was within a theatrical performance.

The combination within a single set of a framed perspective stage and a projecting forestage was a stroke of genius. It allowed Meyerhold both to evoke the material opulence and elegance of the classical stage *and* to exploit the theatrical vitality of the popular stage where Molière's roots lay. And, moreover, to establish a dialectical tension between the two. For Meyerhold's purpose in evoking the seventeenth-century stage was to expose the ideological contradiction

Plate 11 A scene from Meyerhold's production in St Petersburg, 1910, with Y. Yuriev (Don Juan), N. G. Kovalenskaya (Elvire) and K. Varlamov (Sganarelle). One of the proscenium servants can be seen upstage to the left of the picture.

he perceived in *Don Juan.* The contradiction, that is, between the appeal to aristocratic taste and the biting satire of a writer appealing over the head of his patron to a popular public. The stage design thus carried an implicit commentary on the relationship between the Court entertainer and his royal patron.

The production made use of many anti-illusionist devices which were new at the time. The house lights were kept on throughout the performance (as they were in Molière's day) except for the blatantly stagey supernatural scenes. Onstage, hundreds of wax candles were kept burning. Used in combination with electric stage lighting, their yellow flickering light could create an impression of sparkling luxury or a mysteriously atmospheric effect. Meyerhold also used an undisguisedly theatricalist play of light between the different planes of the stage, dimming the lights on the forestage in Act III to create a mysterious *Schattenspiel* or chinese-shadows effect, or darkening the upstage plane for Don Juan's final encounter with the Statue in Act V. For the latter, thunder and lightning emphasised the theatrical nature of the effect.

There was no front curtain to conceal the stage from spectators as they arrived. This was a novelty at the time, though it was not the first occasion Meyerhold had adopted the practice. It can be seen as a natural procedure of theatricalism, which puts the workings of the stage on full view and reminds the audience that what it is seeing is a deliberate presentation. But there was also a more specific reason, to do with the need for acclimatisation. Meyerhold stated that the first task of a director staging *Don Juan* was 'to fill the auditorium with such a compelling atmosphere that the audience is bound to view the action through the prism of that atmosphere'.[15] But, he observed, if the setting is concealed behind a curtain, 'some time is required for the spectator to absorb all the many wonders surrounding the characters on stage. This is not the case with a stage which is open from start to finish... Long before the actors appear on the stage the spectator is breathing in the atmosphere of the period.'[16]

What atmosphere was the spectator to breath in? Everything on the stage was intended to evoke the splendour of Louis XIV's Versailles. In fact, the impression was created without excessive regard for historical authenticity, following Meyerhold's principle of 'free composition'. To evoke the required impression Golovin made use of a deliberate anachronism: 'the stage', he wrote, 'depicted an eighteenth-century (*sic*) palace, elegantly decorated and furnished'.[17] This was because for Russian spectators, the seventeenth century was associated with a still rather rough and unsophisticated late-feudal society rather than a world of polished elegance. The corresponding reference point for Russians would be the court of Catherine II, itself modelled on the French court of the period. The decorations and furnishings were therefore Louis XV rather than Louis XIV. For the same reason the music used in the performance

(*Les Indes galantes* and *Hippolyte et Aricie*) was by the eighteenth-century composer Rameau.

The blackamoors mentioned in Bebutov's account were another anti-illusionist device cleverly integrated into the historical framework. These were six young actors dressed in long flared jackets in powder blue with gold braid, resembling liveried negro attendants from a painting by Tiepolo. Meyerhold called them 'servants of the proscenium'. Inspired by the *kurogo* or stage-assistants of kabuki, they performed their functions in full view of the audience, lighting and extinguishing candles, filling the air with perfume by dropping volatile liquids on to hot metal vaporisers, announcing the interval and ringing silver handbells to summon the audience. Running silently across the carpeted stage like kittens, they collected up the discarded cloaks and rapiers after Don Juan's fight with the brigands, fastened Don Juan's shoe laces and picked up his lace handkerchief when he dropped it. When the Statue appeared in Don Juan's house in Act IV they ran to hide beneath the table. In this way they fulfilled a dual purpose which was partly one of obvious theatricalism and also to contribute to the impression of courtly luxury.

Contemporary observers and later writers have extolled the stunning decorative richness of Golovin's design. But what is generally overlooked is that the entire staging was conceived with a *critical* purpose. As Meyerhold said in connection with the blackamoors, 'all these are not merely tricks for the delectation of snobs, but serve the central purpose of enveloping the action in a mist redolent of the perfumed, gilded monarchy of Versailles'.[18] Not so that the audience should admire, but that they should reflect on the phenomenon of such opulent consumption. The aim, said Meyerhold, was 'to remind the spectator constantly of the thousands of Lyonnais weavers manufacturing silk for the monstrously teeming court of Louis XIV, the Hôtel des Gobelins, the whole town of painters, sculptors, jewellers and carpenters ... all the craftsmen producing Venetian glass and lace, English hosiery, Dutch mercery, German tin and bronze'.[19]

Meyerhold had a special conception of *Don Juan* relating to the author's personal and professional situation in 1665. He saw it as the work of a writer battling for survival at a critical moment in his career: harrassed by enemies, in disfavour with the King, and beset by marital difficulties. He interpreted the play as Molière's riposte against the devout set, against his professional rivals, against the Court – and by implication the King – who together had succeeded in suppressing *Tartuffe.* In the same way that the stage design expressed the ideological tension between Molière the popular entertainer and Molière the Court artist, so the characters were used by Meyerhold to reveal the play's polemical meaning.

The role of Don Juan was built on the concept of a mask, or rather a series of masks. According to Meyerhold, this character was

> a puppet whom Molière uses to settle his score with his countless enemies. He is a bearer of masks: now it is the mask of debauchery, scepticism, cynicism, and the posturing of the gallants of the court of the Sun-King; now it is the mask of the author-accuser, now the mask of Molière himself standing face to face with his perfidious unfaithful wife; now, the mask of the organiser of court entertainments. Only at the very end does he give his puppet the mask of the *Burlador de Sevilla* which he borrowed from the touring Italians.[20]

Meyerhold's idea was to show how Molière manipulated this puppet for a variety of polemical purposes before ironically consigning him to hellfire as the legend required.

The role was given to Yuri Yuriev, an actor who combined youth, intelligence and great physical agility, and one of the few actors at the Alexandrinsky who supported Meyerhold unreservedly from the start. Golovin dressed him as an aristocrat from the court of Louis XIV, in red-and-gold brocade justaucorps with white lace ruffs and blue silk bows, velvet breeches, gold wig, a broad-rimmed hat with blue plumes, and sword on a sash (plate 12). The designer later wrote: 'Yuriev's Don Juan was very young and handsome ... He wore his costume with uncommon, even exquisite, perfection, and was

Plate 12 Yuri Yuriev and Konstantin Varlamov as Don Juan and Sganarelle.

charming, affected to a degree, and modishly urbane – the authentic actor of the time of Louis XIV.'[21] Golovin's use of the word 'actor' is revealing. At this time Meyerhold was already experimenting with techniques to expand the actor's expressive physical vocabulary, which would later be systematised in his theory of biomechanics. Drawing on the idea of 'self-admiration' or 'self-mirroring' borrowed from Chinese theatre, he encouraged Yuriev to develop a stylised form of acting to present the different facets of the role demonstratively. There was no attempt to build a psychologically unified character, but an emphasis on play-acting, significant gesture and rhythm. In speech, too, his aim was to express the masks of the role through a series of 'verbal gestures'. Yuriev himself described his delivery as 'a quick headlong speech, almost without a rise in tone. All my attention was focused on changes of tempo, on rapid, bold transitions from one rhythm to another, on precision of diction, and on different "typefaces" – now speaking in italics, now brevier, now nonpareil, and only very occasionally in bold print.'[22]

Meyerhold saw Sganarelle as an equally important key to the play. Rather than treating the master and servant as a couple, he accentuated the contrast between them. Sganarelle, played by the veteran comic actor Konstantin Varlamov (plate 12), was presented as a figure from farce who embodied folk-wisdom and the judgement of popular opinion. The critic Belyaev compared him to a turkey cock dressed in festive clothes and ribbons, and said he infused the performance with the happy spirit of the 'old theatre'.[23] Yuriev described his first entrance: 'From the depth of the stage Varlamov walks straight towards the audience with his open, good-natured, extraordinarily merry face, without speaking a single word, and his very appearance is so radiant that it seems as if the stage is illuminated in bright light and a holiday has arrived.'[24] As well as cheerfulness and comic naivety, Varlamov-Sganarelle introduced a note of coarseness which carried an implicit comment on the world of Don Juan. In a world of elegant refinement, here was a man who sat down and talked about his digestion or, at the appearance of brigands, ran to the wings to empty his bowels. And while Yuriev-Don Juan adopted distancing techniques to display a series of attitudes, Varlamov-Sganarelle sat on the forestage, looked into the faces of the audience and addressed them directly. Sganarelle did not disguise his criticism of his master, which Meyerhold emphasised by changing some of his lines into addresses to the audience. His remonstration against Don Juan's hypocrisy ('What! You don't believe in anything, and yet you want to pass yourself off as a pious man') was changed to an appeal to the audience: 'Look at that! He doesn't believe in anything, and yet he wants to pass himself off as a pious man.' Meyerhold also gave free reign to the actor's genius for comic improvisation. In the night-time scene he walked along the front of the stage carrying a lantern which he shone into the faces of spectators sitting in the stalls, addressing pleasantries to them. 'It was rather risky', recalled one of the actresses, 'but Varlamov acted with such sincere naivety, and with such unique humour, that nobody took offence.'[25]

In directing the company Meyerhold was aiming for a stylised ballet-like plasticity underpinned by a musicality of rhythm and movement. The entire action evolved according to intricately regulated patterns to which absolute submission was demanded. Initially these methods encountered resistance. Yuriev, however, proved very receptive and after struggling to master the new techniques perfected the dancing rhythms, executed with lightnesss and grace, that Meyerhold was aiming for. His seduction scene with the peasant women was especially admired for its geometrically choreographed dance-like qualities.

There was one striking exception to this: Sganarelle. Varlamov, a septuagenarian doyen of the Imperial Theatre, had no interest in modernist experiments and viewed Meyerhold's arrival with weary scepticism. He announced early on that he knew the part already (he had, in fact, played it twenty years earlier) and would only be attending one rehearsal. When he was finally persuaded to attend, it was immediately apparent that his corpulence and age made it impossible for him to adopt the graceful balletic style of movement. Not only that, but he could not remain on his feet for long. The solution was to install two velvet-covered benches on either side of the proscenium, which was where he spent most of the performance. Varlamov was delighted with the arrangement. All his reservations melted away and he said 'What a director! He doesn't put me upstage in a box set where nobody can see me and I can't see anybody, he puts me right on the proscenium. Everyone was saying "Meyerhold this, Meyerhold that", but he arranged things so that everybody could see me and I could see everyone.'[26]

There was a further difficulty, however: Varlamov was habitually unable to act without a prompt and there was no prompt box on the forestage. Golovin therefore designed two decorative screens with curtained windows, which were placed behind Varlamov's benches. At the start of the play two prompters in costumes and wigs took their places behind the screens, drew back the curtains, and supplied Sganarelle with his lines. Instead of upsetting the balance of the performance, the contrast between Sganarelle's immobility and the graceful agility of the other performers seems to have enhanced the overall effect. Elizaveta Timé, the young actress playing Charlotte, wrote: 'And then a miracle happened. Varlamov was sitting on his bench, all the performers were fluttering around him in precisely choreographed movements, but the impression created was that Sganarelle was exceptionally mobile and alive!'[27]

Undoubtedly one of the reasons for the production's popularity was that the old-timer Varlamov was simply being himself. And yet, his style of acting was completely at odds with that of the rest of the cast. Against Yuriev's finely etched engraving and the filigree work of the ensemble, he was acting with broad, highly coloured brush strokes. In rehearsals this seemed at first to be a major problem. Yuriev was at a loss to know how to relate to his partner. Eventually, however, he realised that a performance could be built successfully on tonal and stylistic contrast. Yuriev then concentrated on playing Don Juan as Meyerhold had demonstrated, leaving Varlamov to make the necessary connection intuitively. And it worked:

'Varlamov's artistic sensibility suggested to him the way to weld our lines together, so that all the while he remained the full master of his spontaneous talent, and did it with such mastery that there was no disharmony between the two of us.'[28]

The production opened on 9 November 1910 and caused a sensation. Four weeks later Telyakovsky wrote in his diary: 'Not one show, I believe, has aroused such interest and so many arguments as *Don Juan.* Every day there is news of various meetings where the production has been discussed by amateurs, artists and professors. Evidently, all St Petersburg has become interested in this.'[29] The opening performance was punctuated throughout by applause, and Meyerhold and Golovin were called to the stage several times. The first reviews were unanimous in praising the play's originality and the perfection of its execution. The critic of the newspaper *Rech* wrote: 'The wonderful festive show, Molière's *Don Juan,* so foreign to the Russian spirit and hidden from us by the melancholic Don Juan of Alexei Tolstoy, rose from the dead and blossomed with magnificent colours. The Alexandrinsky Theatre has here given free reign to artistic innovation, to the creativity of the director's imagination, and this production will enter the annals of our stage as a credit to its directors.'[30]

But soon a polemic developed in which the whole future direction of Russian theatre was deemed to be at stake. In an article ironically entitled 'Ballet at the Alexandrinsky', A. Benois developed a sustained attack on Meyerhold's theatricalism which he regarded as a symptom of cultural decadence. He stated that the ballet-like stylisation of acting reduced the performance to a 'dressy farce', a mechanical charade from which only one actor – Varlamov – was exempt:

> Why did Meyerhold give the role of Sganarelle to Varlamov? It is surely a huge mistake. For in this entire chorus of puppets *there is only one actor...* And what a wonderful actor, marvellous, yes by God's grace a divine actor... When this great Varlamov spoke, no doubt remained that there was a truly great artist whose place is not with the others, simply because the others should not be on a stage.[31]

The critic's central argument was that aesthetic formalism was driving out the essential truth of theatre, which had to be rooted in the human presence of the actor. In Benois's eyes, this confirmed Meyerhold's reputation as a director who reduced the actors to mechanical instruments. It should be noted, though, that this view was not shared by the actors themselves, some of whom had feared initially that they might be reduced to an incidental role.[32]

Another objection, which was voiced by several critics, was that too much importance was given to stage design, and to the stage painter in particular. Benois wrote: 'Golovin is excellent as always. But what has this benefit performance for a scene painter got to do with the resolution of the problem of abolishing scenery?'[33] Another critic called the production 'the triumph of the set without people'.[34] Like directors everywhere in Europe at the time, Meyerhold was engaged in a search for new relationships between actors and setting on a non-illusionist stage. In the long term, as Appia was already demonstrating and as Meyerhold himself later came to realise, the future lay not with scenic decoration and painting, but with architectural solutions treating the stage as a dynamic, non-representational space. His production of Molière belongs to an intermediate period when, in partnership with Golovin, he created a series of sumptuously decorated stages which enveloped the performers. *Don Juan* was the first and consummate example of these 'festive spectacles'.

Despite critical reservations, it enjoyed enormous popular success. With thirty performances in 1910-11 and twenty more in the following season, it survived Varlamov's retirement to be revived again in 1913, 1918, 1922 and 1932. But whether the significance of Meyerhold's interpretation of Molière's comedy was fully grasped at the time seems doubtful. So much controversy was aroused by the revolutionary staging that Meyerhold's intentions regarding the play itself seem to have been overlooked. The production was not *just* a showcase for a modernist theatrical style, nor an exercise in historical reconstruction, but was meant to explore the play's significance in the modern context. This aspect of the production, anticipating

Brecht's approach, was potentially as revolutionary as the staging aesthetic. Meyerhold was the first to recognise the importance of inscribing a dramatic text in its historical framework, and to show that texts belong to a specific past and have to be reconstructed in the present with an awareness of their history, in order to illuminate their contemporary relevance. As a modernist interpretation of a classic, its final originality lay not in the theatrical innovations themselves but in 'the interrelationship between the world depicted on the stage *and the atmosphere of the city where the production was staged*, the atmosphere of Petersburg'.[35] The approach was allusive rather than explicit but the connection was there to be made. Looking back on the period many years later, a Russian critic wrote (not in connection with *Don Juan*): 'Petersburg, reflecting in its bureaucratic population the sun-like play of the throne, was saturated through and through with flippancy, nihilism, scepticism, and irony of empty souls. The theatre was constructed along the same lines.'[36] Sitting in the illuminated auditorium of the Imperial Theatre, its rich decoration mirrored on the stage, and observing the 'perfumed, gilded aristocracy' of Louis XIV, the St Petersburg audience were invited to see a reflection of their world. Most of them, though, chose not to do so. They preferred to see 'a performance [which] was pure joy - the joy of theatre as theatre'.[37]

THE BERLINER ENSEMBLE'S 'DON JUAN' (BENNO BESSON, DIRECTOR)

Volkstheater, Rostock, 24 May 1952

Theater am Schiffbauerdamm, Berlin, 19 March 1954

In the last years of his life, when the central focus of his work was adaptations of classical works presented in a modern critical perspective, Brecht developed the ambition of re-introducing Molière to the German stage. So it was not surprising that, when the Berliner Ensemble settled in the Theater am Schiffbauerdamm in 1954, it was a special adaptation of Molière's *Don Juan* that Brecht chose for the inaugural production. In retrospect, the choice of Don Juan appears virtually inevitable. For Brecht's dialectical theatre, in its various forms, had one overriding purpose: to present spectators with examples, both negative and positive, which demonstrate social reality and the need for social change. And what more negative example is there in all literature than the socially parasitic, obdurate, sexual imperialist and hedonist nobleman, Don Juan? That, at least, was the reading of Molière's play, restored in its historical perspective, proposed to the public of East Berlin.

Brecht was unquestionably the inspiration behind the Berliner Ensemble's *Don Juan*. The key figure in its realization, however, was Benno Besson, who had joined Brecht in 1949 as an actor and assistant director and later became one of the Berliner Ensemble's leading directors.[38] The cosmopolitan Besson, originally from Switzerland, was one of the first theatre people outside East Germany to appreciate the significance of Brechtian technique for the creation of a socially committed theatre. As early as 1946–7, when he was working in Lyon with the French director Jean-Marie Serreau, he adapted and staged Brecht's *A Man's a Man* and *The Exception and the Rule*. While subscribing to Brecht's political and theatrical priorities, he brought to the Berliner Ensemble a uniquely valuable experience of French theatre. In particular, Brecht had high hopes of his knowledge of Molière, which he regarded as being of the utmost importance for the renewal of German comic theatre.

The Berliner's *Don Juan* in 1954 was not, in fact, an original experiment but a re-working of an earlier provincial production. In February 1952 the Volkstheater in Rostock invited Besson to direct Molière's *The Miser* with Norbert Christian in the central role. It was to be his first single-handed production. After considering the idea, Besson made a counter-proposal to stage *Don Juan*, a play more suited to his purposes because, he said, it 'showed a better cross-selection of society of the time'.[39] Moreover, apart from a yawningly reverential production of *Don Juan* at the Kurfürstendamm five years earlier, it had the additional advantage of being virtually unknown in Germany.

In Rostock, Besson already had a good Sganarelle (Norbert Christian) and he was keen to offer the role of Don Juan to Joseph Noerden of the Berliner Ensemble. Besson's first task was to prepare a new German version of the play. This text, which was subsequently adopted for the Berliner production, was a radical adaptation of Molière's play, arranged in four acts and re-written on Brechtian and Marxist principles to bring out the play's social meaning. Hainer Hill of the Berliner Ensemble designed the set and costumes which, again, would be reproduced in the Berliner production. Rehearsals of the first three acts (the final act was not yet drafted) began on 20 April and the play opened four weeks later as part of the Rostock trade unions' theatre week. The entire project, from the first germ of the idea to its realization, had taken just twelve weeks. The première, given for an audience of shipyard workers, was 'greeted with a great deal of laughter and received twenty-two curtain calls',[40] but the production met with reserved critical judgement. Besson's notes from the period suggest that the project was compromised by the difficult material circumstances in which it was mounted, with inadequate resources, inexperienced workers, and limited rehearsal time.

The 1952 performances, which were carefully documented and photographed by Hainer Hill, served as the model for the Berliner Ensemble staging. Rostock thus constituted the real experiment, but one which only came to full fruition when *Don Juan*, now described in the programme as 'an adaptation by the Berliner Ensemble', opened at the Schiffbauerdamm two years later.

One lesson that Besson learned from Brecht, and which he applied to the adaptation of *Don Juan*, was not to be intimidated by the classics. (Or, as the latter preferred to call them, 'old works'). Brecht taught that one should not be afraid to seize the material and re-work it (as Molière did), as long as this helped to reveal the play's original meaning for a modern-day audience. He also refused to be hemmed in by tradition – which, he argued, was in any case a product of modern accretions that masked the sense of the original. Examples, in the case of *Don Juan*, were the idea of Don Juan as a tragic figure, and the idea that he is a revolutionary figure fighting against the old feudal order with militant atheism. Both of these heroic interpretations were dismissed by Brecht and Besson as later bourgeois notions which would have been impossible in Molière's time when such an anti-social figure was seen properly for what he was: in Besson's words, a 'social monster'.[41] For Besson, as for Brecht, it was historically self-evident that *Don Juan* is a comedy and Don Juan himself a comic figure, and no less axiomatic, from a Marxist-historical point of view, that he is a social parasite. These became the twin premises of the Brechtian adaptation.

Many of the changes made to the play thus had as their purpose to expose the un-heroic nature of the central character. A revealing example was the treatment of the scene where Don Juan comes to the aid of Elvire's brother whom he sees being attacked by robbers – a chivalrous act whose motives may be questioned but which may well be seen as casting an admirable light on the hero. There was no such ambiguity in the adaptation where it became a display of craven dishonesty. Don Juan had previously exchanged clothes with Sganarelle. In Molière's play this is proposed but not followed up. The fact that in Besson's version Don Juan does put on his servant's clothes already demeans him. When, subsequently, he sees Carlos being attacked he proclaims, exactly as in Molière: 'The contest is too unequal; such cowardice is more than eyes can bear.' But then Besson makes him add with comic transparency: 'Go to the man's help immediately. Personally I will not fight with such ruffians. Get in there and fight, knave!' Sganarelle's terrified roar as he is shoved into the skirmish scares the assailants who run off, leaving Don Juan to resume his own costume and present himself as Carlos' saviour.

'The prestige of the parasite interests us less than the parasitic nature of his prestige.'[42] Brecht's statement points to their central conception of Don Juan as a corrupt nobleman who ruthlessly exploits his social rank in pursuit of hedonist self-gratification. Along this axis, the other features of the character – his atheism and his sexual adventurism – fall naturally into place. Where his spurious affirmations of atheism are concerned, Brecht's notes make clear in what light they were to be seen:

> Don Juan is not an atheist in the modern sense. His unbelief is not combative: that is, it does not call for any actions. It is simply an absence of belief. It's not a conviction, but simply no conviction at all. Don Juan may even believe in God, but he doesn't want to know about him because that would interfere with his life of pleasure.[43]

The mathematical credo, 'I believe that two and two make four, Sganarelle, and that four and four make eight', far from proclaiming a revolutionary philosophical materialism, was seen as just an empty formula. This was made clear in the production by the bored manner in which it was tossed off. In all the 'philosophical' passages, in fact, Don Juan showed not the slightest interest in engaging in a discussion of ideas, but only weary irritation with a chattering servant who, for the present, had ceased to amuse him.

In the absence of any conviction, it was sexual seduction, which most directors relegate to a subordinate role, that became the *raison d'être* of the Besson-Brecht Don Juan. For it is his behaviour in the field of sexual conquest that allows one to see most clearly how the nobleman uses his social situation to further his personal pleasure. The theme of philandering was reinforced by the introduction of a new character, Angelika, the daughter of the Commander killed by Don Juan, and whom Don Juan was now intent on seducing. At the same time, the text was re-modelled to show that his sexual appetite is not a function of 'character' (i.e. a personal trait) but socially determined (i.e. a function of his position as a nobleman in seventeenth-century France). Don Juan's reference to Alexander the Great in Act I of Molière's play supplied a central motif, that of sexual imperialism. Besson described Don Juan as a *sexuelle Großmacht* – a sexual 'superpower' – but was also at pains to make it clear that his powers of seduction had absolutely nothing to do with personal sex-appeal and were rooted entirely in his social position. With no particular erotic talent, what he does possess in abundance is a combination of determination, stamina, and the total focusing of all his energies on the business of achieving supremacy. In the adaptation, Don Juan brings to the task of conquering women the military strategy that his ancestors applied to the business of conquering countries. For Besson and Brecht, such a portrait of a feudal 'Alexander the Great of Love', with its absurd disproportion between means and ends, could not be other than comic.

Other changes to the play served to expose the class interests inherent in the story. To this end, and to broaden the spectrum of classes represented, a number of new characters were introduced: three boatmen whom Don Juan hires to assist him in the abduction of a young beauty, Marphurius (an old army surgeon), and Serafine (a much put-upon cook). The exploitation and latent violence contained in social transactions were foregrounded in a scene during the first act where Sganarelle was seen haggling with the boatmen over their wages, then instructing them in the way to use their oars as weapons. All this took place upstage in counterpoint to a conversation between Don Juan and his father, who was first introduced in a new scene in Act I. Besson used his interventions to highlight the father's concern at the damage that the irresponsible nobleman is causing to the interests of his own class. Self-interest, not morality, was clearly what impelled Don Louis to act: 'To cover up your scandalous doings I am obliged to wear out the mercy of our king', he complains. The essential point – that his son's scandalous conduct is undermining the right of their class to social hegemony – was exposed even more sharply in Don Louis' second appearance:

> Scoundrel! What is this new exploit I hear of? How contemptible! Am I to cover up such conduct with my name? I no longer can. By what right do you enjoy your privileges? What have you done to deserve the name of nobleman? Have you forgotten how to blush?

> Shall it be said that a nobleman is a monster? Shall it be said that the sons of common labourers are more virtuous than ours? (IV.10)

The final scene of the play brought together all these characters – in fact, the entire company of servants, victims and enemies – who joined with Sganarelle in voicing their impotent anger against the nobleman who had disappeared to hell leaving them all the poorer.[44]

As these examples show, Besson's purpose was to rob Don Juan systematically of any positive or redeeming features, and to do so in such a way as to make clear the dialectical function of the character. Dispossessed of political power and of any productive role in Louis XIV's court, the nobility's parasitic energies are transferred to the pursuit of hedonistic pleasure. With this historical analysis built into the adaptation – and re-inforced by copious historical documentation which spectators received with their programmes detailing the socio-economic conditions of different classes in Louis XIV's France – Besson was able to present German audiences with the first Brechtian production of a play by Molière.

In staging the play his general aim was to create a distancing effect which would allow spectators to maintain a critical perspective. However, the methods he used to achieve this differed from Brecht's usual alienation techniques. As in any Brechtian-inspired production, the audience were not allowed to forget that they were spectators in a theatre and that what they were watching was a demonstration. But this was satire, and it required a different technique from, say, a didactic *Lehrstück* or a historical drama. So instead of breaking down the illusion by interrupting it, Besson adopted an approach which drew on staging conventions of Molière's time and emphasised their artificiality. The basic premise in any Marxist reading of the play is that the vices which Molière painted are not attributes of 'human nature' but products of a specific form of society, and the staging was intended to express this interpretation. The location was not Sicily but France: specifically, the Sun King's court. Even before the play began, the audience were presented with a glimpse of aristocrats at play in a painted front curtain depicting a courtly hunting scene.

When the curtain rose on Hainer Hill's setting, they saw a classically symmetrical stage picture dominated by a painted perspective backcloth which showed a long avenue of poplars leading in the distance to the Palace of Versailles (plate 13). As well as situating the play in its historical setting, the perspective had the effect of diminishing the human figures. On the stage, the line of trees was continued with 'real' trees which formed the upstage wings. Within the permanent setting, different scenes were indicated by balustrades, low hedges or ornate railings placed to form the upstage boundary with, where necessary, other temporary elements such as fishing nets or a chapel. Lest the irony of this elegant historical setting be overlooked, a line of five gilded chandeliers hung above the stage, proclaiming the theatricality of the stage picture.

Thus, instead of adopting Brecht's 'separation of elements' (switching modes and styles), the production appeared to go in the opposite direction of creating a consistent, self-contained theatrical world. The intended effect was the same – to prevent suspension of disbelief – but in order to achieve this Besson relied on the distancing effect of irony and on the consistent partitioning-off of the stage picture behind the proscenium arch.

An analogous principle was applied by the actors who, within the overall theatrical set-up, were not required to distance themselves from their characters. A terse note by Brecht indicates the general direction: 'The play in absolute seriousness, to show how bloody seriously this society takes itself.'[45] Serious, in this sense, is not the opposite of comic but is intended to indicate that the actors should forego self-caricature and rely on the situations to expose them. Besson therefore encouraged the actors to remain within their roles. This is not the same as saying that they played their roles uncritically. On the contrary, Besson required them 'to think about all the actions and attitudes, and to make them visible with corresponding signs'. And he added: 'It did not matter whether the latter were

Plate 13 Hainer Hill's stage setting for the Berliner Ensemble, 1954.

concrete or abstract.'[46] What they did not do, however, was step outside the character to comment on their actions.

A 'light' acting style, as Besson called it, was sought in order to maintain a level of theatrical irony in keeping with the overall production style. Each day before scene rehearsals began, the company improvised a sketch in *commedia dell'arte* style to acclimatise them to the rapid tempo and deft playing which they considered appropriate to Molière's comedy. Music also had an extremely important part to play here. It was used not to link scenes but as background to speech, supplying musical commentary or emphasis in the appropriate style: heroic, melodramatic, lyrical, and so on. The music chosen was by Lully, a contemporary of Molière and fellow court artist who never composed for *Don Juan* but whose style situated the production in the musical context of its time. Besson says that he used the music (for example in Elvire's tirades) principally to help the actress to achieve a light and graceful speech-melody. It is also obvious, however, as Brecht noted in connection with Elvire, that the music undercut the speech in an ironic way and prevented it from acquiring any quality of pathos.

Of the original Rostock cast, only Norbert Christian (Sganarelle) and Lothar Bellag (Carlos) remained. The crucial cast change was the replacement of Joseph Noerden in the role of Don Juan by Erwin Geschonneck. This actor, who had previously played the class-conscious worker Matti in Brecht's *Puntila*, and then the army chaplain in *Mother Courage*, brought exactly the right degree of irony to the role. He had none of the grace often associated with Don Juan and at times, when the boredom of life enveloped him, he appeared almost inert and lumpish. But whenever an opportunity for sexual pursuit energised him, he was transformed into an alert, powerful beast like a hunting lion. What this created, however, was from start to finish a comic Don Juan. By making him the slave to a prompt erection, and by constantly playing on the level of calculation and strategy as opposed to inner experience, Geschonneck adroitly diminished his character. The effect was achieved without crude caricature: the audience's alienation – and hence their evaluation of the character's actions – arose from the overall social context in which he was presented and, of course, from the distancing effect of laughter. And Geschonneck *looked* comic. Strutting about the gardens of Versailles in his pompous costume – a dandified seventeenth-century version of a Roman general's tunic, matched with a wide-brimmed feathered hat and large bows on his shoes – he resembled a plump, middle-aged, self-important turkey-cock (plate 14).

Inverting the common assumption which casts the servant as a buffoon and the butt of his master's superior wit, this production cast Sganarelle as the straight foil to the comic Don Juan. The part was played by Norbert Christian, whose performance as Sganarelle was acclaimed by critics as the actor's greatest to date. His interpretation was original and striking for the level of social realism and insight that he brought to a role which has often been defined mainly in terms of comic tradition. Patiently enduring his lamentable fate like a faithful old dog, he rather enjoyed the advantages of his position: he had an exceptional master which, possibly, made *him* exceptionally interesting, and he had the privilege of a familiarity which allowed him, on occasions, to voice criticisms of his master. Sganarelle's alienation in class terms was shown not only in the long-suffering way he put up with his mistreatment at the hands of Don Juan but also in his relations with fellow servants. In the opening scene, discoursing expansively to Gusman on the virtues of tobacco, feeding Gusman some morsels of information and witholding others, he showed how, in Don Juan's absence, he could enjoy behaving like a master in his own right. A similar effect was repeated in the scene with M. Dimanche and in the new scene with the boatmen where Don Juan delegates his powers to him to hire the men at the cheapest price.

It has sometimes been suggested that Sganarelle is a precursor of Figaro, Beaumarchais' nimble-witted valet who, by his organised resistance to his aristocratic master, announces the spirit of the

Plate 14 Erwin Geschonneck as Don Juan and Norbert Christian as Sganarelle, with Regine Lutz (Charlotte) and Käthe Reichel (Mathurine), Berliner Ensemble, 1954.

French Revolution. There was little evidence in the Berliner Ensemble production of such a view. According to Besson, Sganarelle should rather be seen as standing for 'the oppressed French people who despite their bondage know how to enjoy life and live it so intensely'.[47] Nor, with one exception, was there any suggestion in the other common people of a burgeoning class awareness that things could be other than as they are. Certainly there was none in the pitiful, down-trodden M. Dimanche played by a sweating, ingratiating Hans Hamacher, nor in Charlotte or Mathurine, both materialistic opportunists in their way. If there was a foreshadowing of 1789, it was in the fisherman Pieter (Pierrot), the only character who emerged from the oppressed group to voice a genuine and courageous opposition to Don Juan. His opposition remained impotent, since the purpose of the production was to give an accurate representation of an historical moment (seen, naturally, from a modern vantage point) not to re-write history in a facile meliorist way.

For the same reason, the adaptation retained Molière's ending while emphasising that it is pure contrivance. In comic theatre the unjust receive their deserts, and this is deeply satisfying for the audience. But we are aware, at another level, that it is only in comic theatre that we are afforded the pleasure of poetic justice. To underline this, Besson emphasised that the dénouement is a theatrical trick employed by Molière to resolve what was, in the prevailing social order, an insoluble problem. As Brecht noted:

> In a social order like this there is no authority that can put an end to the parasite except at best heaven – that is to say, theatre machinery. If the stage floor did not open to swallow the shining monster, he would continue to march unhindered and unstoppable through the world.[48]

Besson staged a riotous finale with a gigantic, lumbering cardboard-clad statue, smoke and flames billowing from the stage floor, and a great clamour of shouts. A shooting star passing across the sky added a further ironic touch of convention Throughout it all, to the very last, Don Juan retained the incorrigible fixity of a comic character. The adaptation contains the stage direction: 'With a crash of thunder the earth opens. One hand in the Commander's clasp, *vainly trying to hold his hat with the other*, Don Juan sinks into the depths' (my italics). In the Berlin performance, after Geschonneck had been engulfed in the smoking hole, his hat fluttered out again like a piece of burnt paper, a symbol of human vanity and Don Juan's only legacy to the cheated mortals he left behind.

Presented with such a new and unfamiliar image of Molière, critics were not very sure how to react. On one point they were all agreed: technically, the production was a masterpiece. From a decorative point of view, Hill's elegant setting and precious costumes were very pleasing – perhaps too pleasing – and the skill of the company's ensemble playing guaranteed a wholly unified overall effect. According to one critic, 'Even the smallest and silent roles are critically worked through according to the purpose of the production.'[49] There were innumerable inventive and significant touches in the staging: in the banquet scene, the seating of the musicians up in the branches of the trees; or the duel between Carlos and Alonso, staged as a formal ceremonial in which the young gentlemen were clearly determined not even to scratch each others' skins. Yet, somehow, the performance seems not have touched critics at a deeper level. 'It was beautiful!', one commentator wrote, before concluding: 'Of course, there were neither shocks nor real insight, but it was enchanting and extremely pleasurable.'[50] Another wrote that 'it was not the play on the stage that made the experience, but the play *with* the theatre, in its aesthetic and intellectual perfection, that earned the spectators' applause'.[51]

It is possible that this innovative but neglected production was too ironic, and the approach too unfamiliar in the context of the Berliner Ensemble's style, for its critical charge to be fully appreciated at the time. This is not a criticism that could be made of Besson's later experiments with the play. Since the Berliner Ensemble version he has directed three further productions of *Don Juan*, for the Deutches Theater in 1968 and in Vienna, Geneva and Paris in the 1980s. These later versions, each more outrageously comic than the previous one, will be discussed in the final chapter.

INGMAR BERGMAN'S VARIATIONS ON 'DON JUAN'

Intiman Teatern, Malmö, 4 January 1955
China Theatre, Stockholm, 24 February 1965
Landestheater, Salzburg, 27 July 1983

Like Besson, Ingmar Bergman has long been fascinated by the figure of Don Juan. Over a period of nearly thirty years he has staged three versions of Molière's play, each bearing a distinctive Bergman signature, yet markedly different in tone and overall effect one from the other. The Bergman-Molière Don Juan, in his different incarnations, has always been a tired seducer, a hollow shell of a person mechanically going through the performance of seduction. This central concept, however, has undergone a remarkable mutation over the years. It has lent itself to treatments ranging from the first ironic manifestion (Malmö, 1955), through an engagingly farcical version in *commedia dell'arte* style (Stockholm, 1965), to a toweringly dark vision staged in Salzburg and Munich in 1983.

Bergman's abiding interest in the play mirrors the two defining features of his life's work: an impulse to deliberate theatricality, and a prolonged meditation on the state of contemporary man's soul. To an artist whose work revolves round the metaphysical/ethical/psychological themes of God, guilt, sexuality and angst, the Don Juan legend offers a rich vein of material. Coupled to this is Bergman's admiration – 'veneration' would not be excessive – of the French playwright. Few directors, even in France, have felt a stronger affinity with Molière. To find a comparable case one has to turn to Louis Jouvet, whose approach to Molière in several respects resembles Bergman's. His passion for Molière goes back to the discovery, on his first visit to Paris in 1949, of French classical theatre, an event which he has frequently described as a pivotal moment in his experience of theatre. Greatest of all, he said, was discovering Molière, whom he had previously considered musty and unexciting. It happened at the Comédie-Française, where Jean Meyer was acting in *The Misanthrope* performed at break-neck speed:

> The experience was indescribable. The dry alexandrines blossomed and thrived. The people on the stage stepped through my senses into my heart. I know it sounds ridiculous but that's what it was like. Molière stepped into my heart to remain there for the rest of my life. The spiritual circulation of my blood, previously linked to Strindberg, now opened an artery to Molière.[52]

While Molière's humanist philosophy had a natural appeal to a man of Bergman's outlook, it was the playwright's theatrical genius that he found irresistible, as did Jouvet. Molière, he said, is an artist 'who truly commands the vocabulary of the stage: he is to the very finger-tips a man of the theatre'.[53] Bergman himself has nourished a consuming passion for live theatre since childhood. Despite his reputation outside Sweden primarily as a film director, he continues to regard film-making as an activity but theatre as his life. In Molière he discovered the genius of a writer who combines high artistry with the popular appeal of a showman, superb prosody with unconstrained farce, an unerring pulse and a mastery of the theatrical moment. It is these qualities that have inspired Bergman's productions of *The Misanthrope* (Malmö, 1957, Copenhagen, 1973); *School for Wives* (Stockholm, 1966) and *Tartuffe* (Munich, 1979) as well as *Don Juan.*

Bergman began his professional career in the 1940s working in some of the many excellent provincial theatres in Sweden: at Helsingborg, Gothenburg and then in Malmö where he was artistic director from 1952 to 1960. It was on the smaller of the Malmö City Theatre's stages, the Intiman, that he staged his first *Don Juan.* This was no apprentice piece but a spectacle which combined mature reflection on the significance of the character with the theatrical qualities which were already the hallmark of Bergman's productions: clarity in the overall concept, matched by impeccable precision in the small details.

In staging the playwright for the first time he was acutely conscious, in a way which would perhaps diminish over the years as he absorbed Molière's world into his own, of the continuity of a living tradition of popular theatre. Whatever Molière's art was, he once observed, it was not aesthetic. Here Bergman's approach connects with that of the many directors, starting with Copeau, who have sought to re-theatricalise Molière using performance traditions of the past. 'It is always the popular theatre that saves the day', wrote Peter Brook.[54] (Saves it, that is, from formalised aesthetic systems, preciousness, intellectuality or simply lazy habit and commercialism). 'Rough Theatre', as Brook named it, takes many forms but its constant traits are the proximity of actors to spectators and an absence of what he pejoratively called 'style'. In its modern figurations, of course, it can never be truly artless: a conscious but honest artlessness is the best that can be hoped for. It was in this spirit that, in Bergman's first production of *Don Juan*, there was an appeal to the unsophisticated directness of popular theatre where actors invited audiences to share in the re-telling of old stories and themes.

The approach was reflected first in the setting designed by Stig Nelson. It was not representative of any geographical location or historical period but conjured up an old theatre, perhaps from the time of Molière himself. A raked platform of bare boards was set on the stage floor to form the playing area, with a simple trap-door for the Commander's entrances. Behind it were hung painted canvas backcloths which, an observant critic noted, appeared 'bleached and worn out after having been rolled into bundles and packed and unpacked during month-long tours of the French countryside'.[55] The intention was to give a stylised impression of a seventeenth-century theatre, not an authentic reproduction. Spectators were allowed to see the workings of the stage, albeit in a selective and controlled way. A loop of heavy rope could be seen hanging from the flies, a bulky old wind-machine used for noise effects was visible in the wings, and scene changes were done by costumed actors. Warm, shadowy lighting, as if from the four candle chandeliers hanging above the stage, enhanced the impression of an old theatre.

The use of a platform to make a playing area within the stage is a favourite device of Bergman, almost a signature. It announces the theatricality of the event and creates a privileged space, Bergman's famous 'magnetic point' which he seeks to establish in each production. In the director's words: 'The platform is absolutely the archetypal theatre, the very oldest form of theatre ... [When] the actors climb on to the platform, suddenly they are powerful, magical, mysterious, multi-dimensional.'[56] The platform can best be understood as a point both of convergence (literally, of sight lines) and of outward radiation. The importance it acquires in Bergman's theatrical method derives from his fundamental understanding of the dramatic event as a joint act of creation that occurs between the actors and the spectators.

The theatricalisation of the setting had its counterpart in the theatricalisation of Don Juan's behaviour. The essence of Molière's character as Bergman conceived him was the idea of an actor who constructs the persona of Don Juan the seducer. This guiding concept was made very clear from the start in a striking and original way with a little mime-play in which spectators saw Don Juan create his mask. After the opening dialogue between Sganarelle and Gusman where Don Juan is described as 'a devil, a Turk, a heretic', the spectators were given the suprising sight of a bedraggled, sleepy Don Juan in a short nightshirt. On his head was an absurd comic-grotesque nightcap adorned with red horns, a dual symbol of the cuckold and the devil, which presently was removed to reveal a balding scalp. Yawning, scratching his flea-bites, his voice still croaky, he shuffled downstage towards a mirror and took stock of the damage wreaked by the previous night's debauch. Satisfied with what he saw, he summoned Sganarelle to dress him. Little by little, with the assistance of a black wig and hat, striped court costume, ruff, cloak and sword, Sganarelle transformed the walking hangover into the preening, self-admiring seducer of legend. This dressing-up took place during Don Juan's initial monologue, supplying an ironic counterpoint to his self-justificatory rhetoric. Finally, like Alexander ready to conquer new worlds, he stood admiring his image in the mirror.

At a stroke, Bergman demolished the myth of Don Juan the seducer and in its place showed spectators the un-romantic reality of a self-defeating narcissist trapped in his own created role. The scene with the mirror (one of Bergman's favourite props) effectively suggested the narcissism which Bergman saw as Don Juan's fatal weakness. The great seducer, it suggested, is in reality capable of loving only himself. Just as importantly, the initial pantomime established the persona of the public Don Juan as an entirely artificial contruction, and the image of him unmasked remained with spectators through the rest of the performance. One critic asked: 'What was it that made us see right through Don Juan's noble exterior into his soul in all its corrupt tawdriness?' The answer was: 'Those naked thighs.'[57] The memory of Don Juan undressed, he said, 'follows us throughout the play like an X-ray vision. Don Juan can seduce his victims with his dazzling costumes and gleaming sword, but he can never seduce us.'[58]

Nor could he seduce Sganarelle, who also knew the reality hidden beneath the disguise. The dressing scene provided the key to the subsequent relationship between Sganarelle and Don Juan. It was a relationship completely devoid of illusion. Toivo Pawlo, playing Sganarelle, observed the traditional aspects of the role – the cowardly valet treading a delicate path between subservience and criticism of his master – but gave it all an edge of undisguised contempt. His attitude conveyed none of the awe-struck fascination that often binds Sganarelle to his master, but something close to disgust. Nor did Don Juan make any effort to win Sganarelle's admiration. He merely demanded subservience, imperiously and sometimes violently. When Sganarelle objects to his master's insolent treatment of his father (IV.5), Don Juan menacingly asks him 'I'm wrong?', producing a comic volte-face from Sganarelle. In Bergman's production Georg Årlin actually seized Sganarelle by the throat and throttled him to produce the desired answer. Later in the same act, where Sganarelle steals food from the table, Don Juan held a knife to his throat to make him disgorge it. And in the fifth act, when Sganarelle again wants to speak his mind, it was with a dagger held against his throat that Don Juan forced him to rattle off his pseudo-logical reasoning.

It is always the role of Sganarelle, as confidant, to reveal Don Juan to the audience. Toivo Pawlo fulfilled this function by his frontal playing, taking the audience into his confidence and creating a comic complicity, rather as Varlamov did in Meyerhold's production. But Bergman delved further into the relationship, suggesting that Sganarelle's knowledge of his master makes him a threatening presence to Don Juan himself. The relationship between the two central characters has always been one of the key variables of the play in production. In Bergman's version, the nature of their relationship was determined by the initial scene where Sganarelle had seen his master literally and metaphorically naked. Sganarelle knew – *and Don Juan knew that he knew* – the truth of his master's empty soul. With the other characters Don Juan could affirm his superiority and score effortless victories, but there remained always the residual, poisonous presence of Sganarelle. In psychological terms, Bergman was adopting a practice which he sometimes uses in his films of embodying the protagonist's split psyche in two separate characters. In other words Sganarelle embodied, not Don Juan's conscience (the term is too moralistic) but the self-knowledge that is hateful to him. No doubt this explained why, despite the *lazzi* and playful comic effects that enlivened the action, the play proceeded in an increasingly desperate climate. It also explains why the Commander's Statue and the *deus ex machina* ending could be presented as self-proclaimed theatrical tricks, not to be taken seriously. As agents of retribution they were superfluous: Don Juan's real enemy was himself and the story was one of self-destruction from within.

Despite being the first of Molière's plays to be staged in Sweden in the eighteenth century, *Don Juan* had not been performed there since the 1890s and was not a familiar play in 1955. Critics were curious, but unsure what to make of a production which defied conventional expectations both of the legend and of Molière. Georg Årlin's utterly un-erotic Don Juan perplexed critics. 'It is difficult to know if one should admire or detest Don Juan', wrote one.[59] 'Too much reasoning, too little passion', objected another.[60] Despite reservations about the interpretation, however, the production was praised for the clarity and precision of the staging, its lively tempo and the refreshing *commedia* style. Another critic concluded: 'One left the auditorium with a happy feeling of having witnessed something magnificent.'[61]

Ten years later Bergman revived the play as part of a programme of theatre for schoolchildren organised by the Royal Dramatic Theatre in Stockholm. Bergman was now director of the National Theatre where, as well as directing, his mission included audience recruitment and education. The performances of *Don Juan* were given in a rented variety theatre called China, and the production was also broadcast on educational television. This was a more stylised, playful version of the earlier production, with the accent even more sharply on skilful comic acting in the spirit of *commedia dell'arte*. In addition, the re-creation of a seventeenth-century theatrical performance, already suggested in the original production, now became a central motif. These changes of emphasis, whilst originating in Bergman's desire to re-kindle the essential spirit of Molière, made it an ideal vehicle for introducing young audiences to the pleasures of high-quality theatre. The result, unanimously praised by critics for its outstanding polish and fun, was a performance which combined the exhilaration of well-staged theatre with a gentle lesson in theatre history.

The setting was a modified version of the one designed for the Malmö production. Its centrepiece was the planked platform but this time there were actual footlights at the edge of the stage and the entire scene was framed at the top and sides in billowing drapes,

Plate 15 A scene from Ingmar Bergman's 1965 production (Stockholm).

creating the impression of an itinerant stage set up at Court (plate 15). In this connection, Bergman's treatment of the scenes with Elvire's brothers in a grandiloquent mock-heroic manner is significant. He explained that he wanted to try a pastiche of Molière's troupe parodying the rival company of the Marais.[62] (The idea is not so fanciful, since Molière himself parodies the Marais company's inflated rhetorical style in *The Impromptu of Versailles*). The dénouement combined a spectacular seventeenth-century machine-play effect using sulphur and flames, with a riotous invention of Bergman's where minor characters came onstage and made a raucous noise with rattles, drums and pistols fired in the air.

While following the earlier *mise en scène*, Bergman heightened its playfulness by making more consistent and emphatic use of *lazzi*. On the first occasion when Don Juan held his knife to Sganarelle's throat, for instance, Sganarelle suddenly 'noticed' a letter lying on the floor. With an ad-libbed 'Look what's lying over there', he was able to make a comic escape. Don Juan laughed at the ploy, and the tension was defused. An incident which had contributed a hard edge to the original production thus became an undisguised comic gag, made more ostentatious by the fact that the audience had seen it set up by a costumed stagehand who placed the letter on the floor. The memory of the first gag carried through to the second scene with the knife. This time Don Juan played indolently with the knife, even putting it to his own throat before turning it on Sganarelle. Now, instead of reducing Sganarelle to terrified jibbering, it was the cue for Sganarelle to perform a comic solo number: to Don Juan's amusement, he 'shuffled clumsily around the stage and stammered out the disconnected phrases of his banal reasoning'.[63] Bergman also introduced some new comic business to the fifth-act climax: when hell opened up to receive his master, Sganarelle fled in fear into the auditorium, a time-honoured gag that delighted the young spectators.

In a similar vein, the initial sequence to introduce Don Juan was embellished with numerous additional props, including a chamber-pot, to extend the comic routine. Don Juan was again played by Georg Årlin who was now a decidedly ageing and tired seducer, and his dressing-up included the application of grotesque make-up. Probably the most crucial change was the casting of Ernst-Hugo Järegård as Sganarelle. In harmony with the overall production style he created a brilliant traditional *commedia dell'arte* valet: 'slippery and evasive, cowardly and cunning, an ordinary and frail person who accompanied Don Juan with a good-natured worm's-eye view'.[64] The same critic went on: 'It was a rich, supple performance, marked by good humour and a spirited playfulness, but without depth or seriousness or human pathos.' What was said here of Sganarelle could apply equally to the production itself.

But Bergman had not said his last word on this inexhaustible play. Eighteen years later, in 1983, he returned once more to Don Juan. This third version, which ranks as one of his most powerful theatrical achievements, illustrates vividly how the same basic production concept can be modulated in performance to create utterly different resonances. Again, the staging followed in outline that of the Malmö version. And again, the interpretation centred on the ageing Don Juan. Yet this was no mere revival but a substantially new re-interpretation whose darkness disconcerted many critics. The performance had all the theatrical flair and precision that belongs to Bergman, but it was now a vehicle for a deeply pessimistic and seemingly intensely personal drama of a man confronting his own mortality.

Having left Sweden in 1976, Bergman was now directing at the Munich Residenztheater where, he said, 'there was a brilliant company at my disposal, with Michael Degen as the ageing Don Juan'.[65] Initially Bergman intended that Kurt Meisel, the director of the Residenztheater, should play Sganarelle. When the two men fell out, he brought in Hilmar Thate from East Germany to replace him, an actor who proved an ideal foil for Degen's Don Juan. Bergman also had an outstanding veteran, the nonagenarian Erwin Faber, to play Gusman. The production, in Heinz Schwarzinger's German translation, opened at the Salzburg Festival in July 1983 before going into repertory at the Residenztheater that autumn.

In Bergman's theatrical principles, it is always the actors who create the drama, or rather, the actors in partnership with the audience. Drama, for Bergman, is an imaginative and emotional experience that is forged in the interaction between actor and spectator. 'A theatre performance', he has said, 'is a matter of give and take. It is in their hearts, in their imaginations that the performance must take place. Because there are only three things necessary for a performance to work: the play – the words – the actors, and the audience. Everything else is absolutely unimportant.'[66] These principles were reflected in the setting for the new production, now pared down to the barest essentials. Designed by Gunilla Palmstierna-Weiss, it followed the familiar principle of a raked platform of bare boards which was framed, in this production, by the walls of the theatre itself. All that was needed to complete the setting were a few indispensable pieces of furniture (a simple wooden table and chair) and temporary screens placed upstage (for example, a line hung with sheets for the second act) for decor. Less constrained by the motif of historical reconstruction, it supplied a timeless and highly flexible theatrical space.

In approaching the play for the third time, Bergman was increasingly sensitive to the fact that, beneath the somewhat desperate clowning, the comedy masks a darkly introspective drama. In a programme note for the Munich production he alludes to Molière's personal and professional struggles, and describes the play thus: 'A fairy tale. But one in which the princesses disintegrate into skeletons. It is hard to imagine the depth of despair in which Molière wrote this play.'[67] On another occasion he said the author of *Don Juan* was: 'a man who has felt the pain of death and at the same time is obsessed by his love of life. So, when all is said and done, it is really a play about life and death.'[68] Despite the magic of its poetry and humour, despite the life-affirming forces it contains, it seemed to Bergman a play where Molière's bitterness seeped into every corner, thwarting every aspiration towards fulfilment. Although the action centres on the last twenty-four hours in the life of the doomed hero, it is, he noted, a play in which everyone loses something that is important to them, be it their wages (Sganarelle, M. Dimanche), their self-respect (Don Louis, Don Carlos, the Beggar) or their chance of love (Elvire, Charlotte, Mathurine, Pierrot).

As for the central character, Bergman stated: 'Don Juan is a totally negative person. He is already an exhausted man whose only pleasure lies in manipulating other people.'[69] This new version turned the spotlight on the sick-at-heart anti-hero as never before. As in the previous productions, the spectators' first sight of him was the unromantic image presented in the dressing scene. But now the pantomime had lost its earlier quality of a farcical charade to become a grotesque and chilling death-invoking ritual. From the start of the play Don Juan's splendid costume could be seen hanging on a tailor's dummy. Following the expository dialogue with Gusman, Sganarelle drew a screen aside to reveal his master asleep, covered, as the Markers described it, 'with an ornate black-and-gold brocade cape like a corpse on a *lit de parade*'.[70] Then began the resurrection as Sganarelle and La Violette transferred the Don's court costume from the mannequin to the living cadavre who stood facing the audience with a blank stare. What Michael Degen communicated was not Don Juan's narcissistic self-satisfaction but his terminal weariness and utter revulsion at the role he must enact. Despite Bergman's reference to him as 'an ageing Don Juan' he was not an old man in the physical sense, far from it; what was shocking was that his eyes were those of a man already dead inside.

Erotic desire had long since ceased to interest him, a point made with brutal clarity in the two scenes where he met Elvire. In the first of these, again in the Markers' words: 'Elvire's angry recriminations were met by Don Juan with neither deceitfulness nor with unkindness – his face as he listened, eyes closed, was a shuttered mask that barely concealed his revulsion.'[71] Their final encounter – a fleeting glimmer of erotic arousal, quickly extinguished – was used to convey a definitive expression of Don Juan's withdrawal, not just from sex but from life itself. After Elvire's exit, Don Juan stared for a moment at her discarded cloak on the floor where it had dropped when they embraced. Then, in a superb theatrical gesture of finality, he picked the cloak up and slowly and deliberately dropped it over the edge of the stage.

Intriguingly, all the energy and virility traditionally associated with Don Juan were transferred in this production to his servant. Hilmar Thate's Sganarelle was as warm-blooded and vital as Degen's Don Juan was saturnine and empty. The encounter with Charlotte and Mathurine in the second act was acted as a racy seduction scene. This certainly made a refreshing change from the Marivaudesque pastoral that it sometimes is. What gave it its point, however, was that the part of the womaniser was played by a lusty Sganarelle who had exchanged clothes with Don Juan. As he performed his master's seduction routine he was watched from upstage by a ghost-like Don Juan. It was an extraordinary and audacious inversion on Bergman's part of the conventional situation. Sganarelle's life-affirming enjoyment of the situation was certainly part of the picture. So too was the irony that the gullible women were being doubly duped, since it was not even the rich nobleman, as they believed, that was seducing them. And hovering behind them, Don Juan was subjected to the humiliation of watching his servant perform a role he is unwilling or unable to perform. Or was it vicarious pleasure that he felt? Michael Degen's lifeless mask made it impossible to tell.

Don Juan thus moved through the play like an animated corpse so that the ending, when it came, seemed like a longed-for release from life. Bergman imbued his death with a provocative mixture of tenderness and shocking brutality which lifted it far above the theatrical convention of a machine-play dénouement:

> As four spectral figures, each wearing a grinning death mask, appeared on the balconies overlooking the stage and called the offender to repentance and reckoning, the compassionate Sganarelle rushed impulsively to Don Juan's side and held him in a close, protective embrace. During a long, dream-like instant of suspended time, servant and master merged into a single, extraordinary figure, hurling painfully slow, hallucinatory gestures of defiance at the four spectres. Then abruptly, like someone drained of life, Don Juan collapsed in Sganarelle's arms as the stone statue of the Commander broke in on them.[72]

The Statue (plate 16) made its dramatic entrance by bursting through a carton-paper screen. Bergman has suggested that the Commander can be seen almost as a forgiving figure as he draws Don Juan down to hell where he already belongs. 'How pleasant it must be', he wrote, 'to burn from the outside rather than from the inside.'[73] From which the logical conclusion to be drawn must be that Molière makes hell a place of redemption. It was little wonder, he noted, that a contemporary was prompted to say that 'Molière must be a devil in human disguise'.

Plate 16 Final scene from Bergman's 1983 production (Salzburg).

Like Jouvet, Bergman claims to detest the intrusive presence in a performance of an ostentatious director. For himself, he said, 'I cannot and will not direct a play contrary to an author's intentions. And I have never done so. Consciously I have always considered myself as an interpreter, a re-creator.'[74] He modestly refutes the idea that his stagings of Molière are a 'renewal' of the ancient texts: 'No, not at all. My intention is not to be a renewer. I want only to present the plays and to make them live in the hearts of the audience. That is my only intention.'[75] Such remarks, like all directors' claims to be faithful to the play, should not be taken too literally. Bergman's art, after all, is also an intensely personal statement. Moreover, his *Don Juan* clearly represented a re-shaping of the play, if only in choosing to ignore certain dimensions. The truth is that Bergman has offered spectators his version of *Don Juan*, which is as it should be. His particular contribution to the stage tradition of Don Juan is to have explored the vertiginous depths of his emptiness and exposed his existential bankruptcy with painful acuity. Over the years he has developed that vision and in his latest, darkest version, brought his weary Don Juan to the point where his final end is not even a suicide but merely the formal acknowledgement of his inner deadness. 'If one can believe in God, there is no problem', says a character in Bergman's film *The Prison*. 'If one cannot, there is no solution.'

AN ABSURDIST 'DON JUAN' IN PRAGUE (JAN GROSSMAN, DIRECTOR)

Na zábradlí Theatre, Prague, 1989–1992

In former Czechoslovakia, *Don Juan* is associated above all with the name of Jan Grossman, one of the leading figures of the Czech stage from the 1960s until his death in 1993. His three productions of the play, first seen in Hradec Kralové in 1982 and later in Prague, were conceived during the period of so-called 'Normalisation', the official designation for the re-imposition of Communist control after the invasion by Warsaw Pact forces in August 1968. Against this background his absurdist and avowedly Camusian interpretation offered an astringent commentary on the existential difficulty of living in a manifestly abnormal society.

His production was the culmination of many years' reflection on the Don Juan theme and, more broadly, of the experiences of an artist-intellectual in Communist Czechoslovakia. It would not be excessive to say that Grossman, a critic and theorist by formation, was driven into the profession of director by the regime's hostility to his work.[76] As a young lecturer in the post-war years of freedom, he had emerged as a prominent spokesman for a group of left-wing poets before being expelled from the university after the putsch of

1948. Permitted to work in the provinces as critic and literary adviser, he published an important theoretical study of Alfréd Radok, the outstanding director of post-war Czech theatre, whose theatrical ideas would influence Grossman's own work when he began directing. During the 'thaw' (the relative easing of ideological control under Krushchov after 1956), he was able to return to Prague as editor at the Czech Writers' publishing house, before falling into official disfavour again. With other intellectual avenues becoming increasingly closed to him, he gravitated towards working full-time in the theatre in the late 1950s.

Grossman's entry into directing coincided with the start of a renaissance of Czech theatre. This was possibly because of, rather than despite, the material and political difficulties confronting artists under a controlled ideological regime. As one Czech critic observed:

> Good theatre needs a delimited space in which to thrive. Absolute freedom kills it as surely as absolute lack of freedom. The 1960s constituted such a space, in which a certain degree of freedom, albeit one whose continuation was constantly in doubt, allowed the development of the most powerful drama imaginable: the struggle between a creative intellectual force and a repressive political force.[77]

Jan Grossman was one of a number of influential figures who came into this environment, mostly from non-theatrical backgrounds, around 1960. Dedicated to avant-garde experiment, but driven above all by moral and political imperatives, they aimed to create an alternative to the official theatre and were openly opposed to the governing Communist ideology. It was their progressive artistic–political aspirations that led to the development of the so-called 'small theatre' movement which flourished in Prague between 1958 and 1968. One such venture was the Divadlo Na zábradlí (Theatre on the Balustrade), founded in 1958 as an experimental studio theatre by Ivan Vyskocil and Vladimír Vodicka (a psychologist and lawyer respectively). It was to this theatre that Grossman, who by now had a small number of highly regarded productions to his credit, came as director in 1962.

The next six years were to be a golden age for the Na zábradlí Theatre. Grossman devoted himself to introducing Prague audiences to the European repertoire of absurdist writers and their precursors, with Czech premières of Jarry's *King Ubu*, Beckett's *Waiting for Godot*, the short early plays of Ionesco, and Grossman's own adaptation of Kafka's *The Trial*. He also worked with the young Václav Havel whose early plays were all premièred at the Na zábradlí in the 1960s. As well as introducing an original repertoire, Grossman stamped the company with a distinctive production style. Inspired partly by Radok's principles and dubbed 'appellative theatre', its emerging hallmarks were a concentration on essentials and a sharp, precise delineation of meaning expressed by a limited number of concrete motifs – all features which would characterise the later production of *Don Juan*.

The invasion in 1968 and subsequent departure of Grossman and Havel brought an end to this exciting period, and with it Grossman's involvement at the centre of Czech theatrical life. After spending a number of years directing abroad, he was permitted to work only in provincial theatres or in the controlled environment of Party-run theatres in the Prague suburbs. It was not until early in 1989, a few months before the 'Velvet Revolution', that the increasingly disillusioned and pessimistic director was able to return to the Na zábradlí. His opening production, enthusiastically acclaimed as a triumphant come-back, was the revival of *Don Juan* first staged in the relative obscurity of Hradec Kralové.

Illustrating the dictum that theatre is often more profoundly political when it avoids direct political comment, the production was oppositional in a social and political sense, but it achieved this in a complex and often ambiguous way. The interpretation was especially unusual in the tragic portrayal of the central character. Whereas most Eastern European productions have directed their critical charge at Don Juan himself, Grossman's used him as an agent of attack on the spectators' consciousness. Like Camus' Don Juan and Caligula, he is penetrated with an awareness of the absurd. He knows there is no meaning in a world without God, and that death is the only reality. Devoid of illusions, there remains only the possibility of distraction. In an echo of the Camusian ethic of quantity – the multiplication of experience which motivates Don Juan's sexual profligacy – Grossman makes him declare: 'Change is everything – all the rest is boredom, sleep, dying.' For a while, Don Juan finds distraction in his encounters with other characters on whom he turns a wearily sceptical eye. Each of these in their way is caricatured as a mask: Elvire's mask of the wronged wife concealing the spite of a rejected lover, the peasants' acquisitive materialism, the absurd pomposity of an anachronistic nobility, and so on. But Don Juan readily penetrates their masks, and each encounter only reinforces his contempt for their inauthentic lives. Alone among the characters, he is interested only in the truth. Quoting Camus, Grossman said: 'Don Juan has chosen: he does not want to be anything. He just wants one thing: to see clearly.'[78] Although his piercing vision can inevitably lead only to hopeless resignation, he nevertheless attains a kind of dignity in his lucidity as he waits for death.

The production was preceded by extensive re-modelling of the text. As a dramaturg Grossman's purpose was not to interpret Molière (he confided only semi-jokingly that he was attracted to this play because he disliked Molière)[79] but to take the play as a starting point for a script which suited his purposes. The action was substantially re-shaped. There was no Statue, no *deus ex machina*; the characters and their motivation were re-defined; the social environment was modernised, aristocratic titles were eliminated and the language was simplified; speeches, and even whole scenes, were cut and re-ordered, and fragments of other texts were inserted – François Villon especially, though there were also echoes of Brecht, Camus and the absurdists. The result was a terse, elliptical text and a more compact drama, with a running time of under two hours including interval. It amounted virtually to a new version of the play, precisely fashioned to the director's personal vision and the social climate in which it was created.

One structural change which greatly affected the sense of the production was the elimination of the topographical variety and episodic time-frame which characterise the original play. In Molière's version three exterior locations, where we witness Don Juan's escapades in the world at large, are followed by a closing of the net in the last two acts. That structure, resembling a dramatic journey, creates an illusion of freedom initially, though we see at the end that Don Juan's 'liberty' was a self-deception and that the entire action is a journey towards an appointed end. Grossman's characters, in contrast, existed throughout in a closed space, in undifferentiated time, with the end – Don Juan's death – symbolically represented on the stage from the beginning. The motif of a journey was replaced by a Beckettian waiting, in a world of decay and stagnation, for a Statue that never comes.

To represent this imaginary world, Ivo Žídek designed a stage embodying an image of death and a near-terminal state of suspended time (plate 17). Almost filling the small stage was the fractured, peeling shell of a crumbling tomb, a towering hollow pyramid set on a raised platform. Neither realistic nor wholly abstract, but concrete and symbolic, the stage presented spectators with a constant image of death and decay. It also served as an acting machine, with all the action taking place on, in, or around the tomb-like structure. Entrances had to be made through the narrow passages beside the tomb, or by clambering over the pedestal and down steps or a ramp to the stage floor, or through a broken hole leading down to the hollow space beneath the tomb. Don Juan and Sganarelle had mastered the space completely, the former languidly circling its contours or reclining on its flat surfaces with his eyes closed, the latter manipulating the space acrobatically. It thus came to be seen as 'their' world. But for their pursuers it was a series of pitfalls and traps into which they were lured by the protagonists, or an obstacle to be negotiated with difficulty, and even an unmasking device in the way that it made it hard for them to maintain their dignified posture.

Plate 17 A scene from Jan Grossman's *Don Juan* (Prague, 1989). Jiří Bartoška (Don Juan), Jana Preissová (Elvire), Ondřej Pavelka (Sganarelle).

Along with the elimination of the varied scenic locations there were also textual changes which served to focus the action on Don Juan's experience. At the end of the first act, for example, after Elvire's exit, Molière switches directly to Pierrot and Charlotte, creating the impression that the peasants inhabit an autonomous world into which Don Juan will later intrude. In Grossman's version, however, a short dialogue linked the scenes. Sganarelle, in an approving comment on Don Juan's adroit dismissal of Elvire, said 'Curtain. Applause'. Don Juan replied: 'And the beginning of a new scene. How shall we do it...?' and went on to announce his plan to separate Charlotte from Pierrot. Only then did the peasant characters appear, re-inforcing the sense that all the characters existed only through Don Juan's critical gaze.

In the 1989 production the title role was played by Jiří Bartoška, a star performer who excels in young male leads on stage and television. His remarkable Don Juan, broodingly handsome with his face set in a cold mask of boredom and contempt, was one of the memorable creations of recent Czech theatre. It was Bartoška who gave the production its pervasive atmosphere of overwhelming, almost intolerable, weariness. Grossman dressed him in black leather trousers and jacket and a black leather cloak, a theatricalist costume but suggestive of the nihilism of a lost generation of disaffected youth. Sganarelle wore black leather trousers like his master, but a yellow satin blouse denoted a less introverted character. Ondřej Pavelka played him not as a buffoon but as a servant eager to please. Although seemingly confident at first, his hollow eyes gave him a haunted look which increased as the action proceeded.

The play was in two parts, the first modelled quite closely on the action of the first three acts in Molière's play. But the extent of Grossman's re-working of the text was already evident in the opening scene. Instead of a put-upon valet who complains to a fellow servant about the scandalous conduct of his master, one saw a self-possessed Sganarelle who was totally identified with Don Juan. The tone of his narration of Don Juan's recent adventures was changed to one of admiration, with all its famous criticisms of his master removed. He listened knowingly to Gusman's description of Don Juan's behaviour, broke in to supplement it with evident approval, and concluded the account of his latest conquest with a triumphant 'It was terrific', before despatching Gusman with a shove. The second scene, between master and servant, confirmed that the polarity in this production was not between Don Juan and Sganarelle but between the couple and the rest of the world. The speeches where Sganarelle reproaches Don Juan were removed, whilst the latter's monologues were given as dialogue in which the characters appeared to be reinforcing a shared view of the world. The scornful dismissal of sexual fidelity, for example, was spoken by Sganarelle on Don Juan's behalf. But if the ambivalence that we see in Molière's Sganarelle was replaced by total complicity with his master, their relationship was far from being one of equal companions. In Sganarelle Grossman depicted another form of false existence, the inauthenticity of the weak who cleave to the point of view of the stronger. As Don Juan's alter ego, Sganarelle seemed to mirror his every thought, but in a purely reactive way. It was the behaviour of a pragmatist who survives at the expense of his own identity.

The encounters with other characters which make up the remainder of the first two acts developed the theme of the mask, and with it the idea of inauthenticity. Like Don Juan, a man with a compulsive need to act out his life in front of others, these characters were all presented as actors playing a role, a point underlined by the stylised elements of period costumes they wore. But while for Don Juan acting is a catalyst to expose the truth (another Camusian idea) his adversaries were presented as the bearers of social masks which Don Juan rips off to lay bare the inner hypocrisy. The first meeting with Elvire resembled some ritual court dance where recent lovers exchange cold civilities. Jana Preissová's Elvire caricatured indignation and offended pride with a haughty stance and the precise steps and swirling movements of a bullfighter. The brightly-lit peasant scenes were also performed like a dance, but this time a stylised country dance. Pavel

Zedníček as Pierrot in the 1989 production, was an energetically physical clown playing lazzi for broad comic effects. (In the 1992 revival a different effect was created when the role, now played by Jan Hrušínský, was interpreted as a naive and gentle pastoral figure, more reminiscent of Watteau than *commedia dell'arte.* The result was not to make the comedy more sentimental, of which there was never a trace in Grossman's production, but to emphasise the tragedy of human manipulation). These episodes served as shafts of light penetrating the predominantly dark production, but without departing from Grossman's overall interpretation. The easily manipulated Pierrot, and Charlotte's slightly mechanical movements, with floppy limbs like a rag-doll and sudden peals of laughter, gave the impression of an absurd comedy of vanity and gullibility enacted by puppets. In all these encounters, Don Juan seemed to be trying to provoke a truly human response and finding none.

The third act was already markedly darker in tone than Molière's and was played on a dimly lit stage. It began with Sganarelle reciting two verses of Villon's astonishingly caustic 'Ballad of spiteful gossips'. During most of the philosophical exchange which follows (III.1) Don Juan remained broodingly laconic, until Sganarelle's reasoning led him to fall down. Whereupon, in place of the traditional statement of the obvious, Don Juan commented darkly: 'And to remain lying. First on the ground, then underneath it.' It was only now, at the end of their discussion, that he delivered the famous credo 'I believe that two and two make four', to which Grossman added an afterthought: 'But even doing this simple operation we are lost.' At the literal level the words referred to the fact that the characters had lost their way in the forest. But their symbolic meaning was clear enough to the audience. As one reviewer put it:

> From Jiří Bartoška's interpretation we can see very clearly that even this simple mathematical truth can be unbelievably manipulated. When even something as trivial as this cannot be believed, how can we take any other principles seriously?[80]

Compounding the ironic ambiguity, Don Juan pointed towards the approaching the Beggar and told Sganarelle: 'Try asking that fellow over there which way we should go.'

The ensuing incident where a bedraggled beggar, naked save for a loin-cloth, is the subject of experimental verification of Don Juan's scepticism, was pushed to the very limits of black comedy. Don Juan brandished a roll of banknotes in his face and, inviting him to foreswear his faith, he proceeded to set fire to the money. When the beggar, writhing in torment, his words choked, attempted to grasp the money, Don Juan first planted his foot on the man's wrist, then released it. The scene was executed with deliberate ambiguity, making it impossible to tell whether the man had succumbed or not. Less ambiguous, however, was Don Juan's parting shot, changed by Grossman from Molière's 'I give it to you for the love of humanity' into: 'You can take it, since God has abandoned you.'

Ambiguity pervaded the climax of the third act, where Molière's Don Juan meets the Statue. In Grossman's version there was no visible Statue, but its effect was felt through the gravitational pull of the ever-present tomb. At the climax of the first part, spectators entered the imaginary space of the tomb by means of amplified voices played through an echo chamber when first Sganarelle, then Don Juan himself, peered into its depths and invited the Statue to supper. What they saw in the tomb one could not tell. Probably nothing, because, unlike Molière's Don Juan who reacts with defiance to the sign from the Statue, the absence of any response from the tomb seemed to accentuate Don Juan's despair. Wrapping his cloak around him as if he suddenly felt cold, he said 'Let's go.' Here Grossman's version added the words 'Everything's boring now', recalling Don Juan's earlier statement that 'Change is everything – all the rest is boredom, sleep, dying.' With these words Grossman replaced Molière's image of an unrepentant sceptic with one of resignation, the bitter resignation of a man who has seen through the sham of moral retribution.

The changes in the second half were more radical. Acts four and five of Molière's play were collapsed into a continuous sequence of twelve scenes with a running time of thirty-five minutes. It began with the usual succession of visitors: M. Dimanche, Don Louis, Elvire. But instead of bringing entreaties, warnings and an eleventh-hour chance of redemption, these encounters were written and staged to vindicate Don Juan's diagnosis by providing final confirmation of the moral vacuity of the world. A stiffly preposterous M. Dimanche, decked in an outlandish green and white striped Court costume, was played off with humourless cynicism by Don Juan. Don Louis delivered an abbreviated tirade on duty. It was recited unconvincingly as a hollow form of words which he no longer believes, and received by Don Juan in contemptuous silence. Elvire re-appeared, but not, in this version, to urge him to repentance. Beneath a penitential black cloak one saw a glimpse of brilliant red. The cloak slipped to the ground to disclose a revealing scarlet dress and a silver crucifix which she later brandished like a weapon. There followed a playback scene where the characters re-lived their first courtship against the sound of their own recorded voices, the first and only sensuous moment of the entire performance. Embracing her from behind, Don Juan seemed wearily to be trying to re-kindle his passion. Suddenly sensing its futility, he tore the crucifix from her neck and in a flurry of indignation Elvire was gone.

At this point the Statue should arrive. But there was no fourth visitor. At the climactic moment of Molière's fourth act there was now an absence. The programme again quotes Camus: 'Above all, I believe the Commander did not come that night, and that as midnight passed the unbeliever was forced to experience the terrible bitterness of those who are proved right.' For Grossman, as for Camus, the true tragedy of Don Juan is that the Commander, the embodiment of absolute morality, did not come, because it could not exist. Don Juan, Camus asserted, 'would willingly accept punishment. Those are the rules of the game. And his generosity lies precisely in his acceptance of the rules of the game. But he knows he is right and that it is not a question of punishment. Destiny is not a punishment.'[81] Since there is no truth, no morality and no punishment, all that remains for him is to consummate the futile comedy of, in Camus' words, 'a life penetrated through and through with the absurd'. Like Camus' hero, Bartoška's Don Juan now prepared himself for death, a death which is not hoped for but accepted with resignation. But while Camus envisaged Don Juan living out a protracted wait into old age in a state of continuing awareness of the absurd, Grossman's version now moved rapidly to its conclusion.

On Elvire's exit, Sganarelle entered carrying two flaming torches (a textual echo of Molière's play: '*Don Juan* – Take this torch; *Commander* – Those who are guided by the divine light have no need of torches'). On a darkened stage, Don Juan and Sganarelle performed a frenzied display with the torches, part-juggling, part-fight, to the accompaniment of the dramatic chanting of the first section of *Carmina Burana.* These chilling acrobatics supplied the necessary theatrical climax to fill the void of the absent Statue and signalled that the action was entering its final phase. As a commentary on the meetings with the three visitors, it expressed Don Juan's strange mixture of exasperation, desperation and manic elation. The father's second visit was reduced to the briefest minimum. Seeing him enter, Don Juan knelt in prayer clutching the crucifix left behind by Elvire (plate 18). The mere gesture of his son's hypocritical piety was sufficient to satisfy him – not because he is gullible but because he lives in a world where outward confirmity is all. No one need be fooled, provided the appearance of re-integration into the system has been satisfied. This lent a new and pungent topicality to the speech on hypocrisy which Don Juan now delivered in its entirety. In another significant textual addition, he concluded his tirade against hypocrisy with the words: 'These times are rotten, dear Sganarelle, and no other times will be forthcoming for some time.' This was not given as a justification of his own hypocrisy, as it sometimes is, but as a way of crystallising the reality of the situation. The scene where Elvire's brothers reappear and challenge Don Juan was cut short by the latter praying, an explicit detail which seventeenth-

Plate 18 Vlastimil Bedrna (Luis) and Jiří Bartoška (Don Juan) in another scene from Grossman's 1989 production.

century censorship would not have permitted. Comically, the two brothers were stopped in their tracks by the word 'Oremus!' and adopted a position of prayer as if by conditioned reflex.

The dénouement was entirely of Grossman's invention. First, Elvire's brothers were despatched to a fittingly absurd and melodramatic death. Moving in to attack, Alonso lunged towards Sganarelle, was repulsed and, turning, fell into an embrace with Carlos in which each impaled the other. Under Don Juan's impassive gaze, Sganarelle, now filled with horror and fear, strove to conceal their bodies in the hollow base of the tomb, collected up their discarded weapons, then stood in helpless silence looking down at his master. Suddenly energised, Bartoška hurled himself towards the tomb (or at Sganarelle who stood in his path?), ran on to the blade which Sganarelle was still holding, and slumped to the ground. All these movements were rapid and confused, creating a calculated ambiguity which left the audience unsure whether they had witnessed a murder, a suicide or an accident. Clearly, Grossman's interpretation allowed no room for divine justice, nor even an immanent social justice. The staging allowed one to conclude, as one critic wrote, that Don Juan went to his death deliberately because 'he has seen too much, too clearly'.[82] However, Grossman's assistant, Aleš Kisil, spoke of 'the murder of Don Juan' and said: 'Sganarelle must get rid of him because he is the highest representative of a society which Sganarelle, in the name of his new utopian reality, must destroy.' And he added: 'Here Sganarelle's moral principles coincide with those of modern terrorists: it's not the murderer who is guilty but the murdered.'[83] The killing of Don Juan, Kisil implied, represents the behaviour of someone who knows he has sold himself and is afraid: in other words, another inauthentic action carried out with the hope of achieving re-integration in the social system.

The final message of the production, however, lay not so much in the manner of Don Juan's death but in the chilling parody of a curtain call which followed it. As Sganarelle turned to the audience, appealing for sympathy or understanding, the other characters loomed into sight upstage and marched forward slowly and mechanically like statues to the sound of an unpleasant noise like crunching gravel. It was as if the Statue had been eliminated from the action only to appear at the end, multiplied ten-fold, to close ranks over Don Juan's corpse. The re-appearance of these characters supplied a concretisation of the social order which in Molière's text is evoked only verbally in Sganarelle's epilogue. The audience's last sight was of the phalanx of statues staring at them with dead eyes and challenging them to react.

'Theatre of the absurd', wrote Grossman in a study of Kafka's theatricality, 'is analytical and coldly diagnostic.'[84] These are terms which could be applied to his production of *Don Juan*, a production which was as economical with humour as it was uncompromising in its bleak vision of society. However, this description overlooks the rich satisfaction afforded by Grossman's theatricality and his extraordinary ability to create theatrical meaning through the deployment of a small number of carefully chosen elements. A typically precise lighting design employed sharp, predominantly white, lighting to introduce tonal contrasts to the darker moments. With similar precision the production employed recurrent musical motifs from Orff's *Carmina Burana* cantata: the urgently chittering strings section to announce Elvire's appearances, the lively dance movement to introduce the peasant scenes and the dramatic chanting of the plainsong accompanying Don Juan himself.

Rigorous textual analysis; a concrete stage space which is both metaphorical and dynamic; directing that is economical, sharp but richly suggestive; delineation of social masks by means of gesture and costume; striking musical motifs: these constituted Grossman's distinctive 'signature' in *Don Juan.* The result was a theatrical transcription of an idea which was simultaneously complex, ambiguous and precise, and it was primarily this that gave the production its intellectual and imaginative appeal. Despite the absence of specific temporal and social reference, however, the production never lapsed into the total abstraction that was a feature of earlier absurdist drama. There was no attempt to evoke the Sicily of the legend, nor seventeenth-century France nor indeed any recognisable time or place. The characters existed only in the fictitious world of the stage. Yet, somehow, the resulting picture retained the sense of a real situation which allowed spectators to relate it to their own experience.

The highly acclaimed revival in 1989 should have remained in repertory for a long run but circumstances determined otherwise. Following Grossman's return to the Na zábradlí, a rift had developed with actors who remained loyal to his predecessor Evald Schorm, the director who had kept the company together during the 1980s. In November 1991, when *Don Juan* was being performed on tour in Rezno, a number of actors abruptly quit the company. Rather than abandoning the production, Grossman's reaction was to recruit a new cast. It was a sign, perhaps, of the importance he attached to it as a personal and artistic statement. Accordingly, *Don Juan* opened again in July 1992 in an almost identical *mise en scène*. From the 1989 cast, only Jan Přeučil's Carlos and Ondřej Pavelka's outstanding Sganarelle remained. Don Juan was now played by Jan Novotný (who had created the role of Sganarelle in the 1982 production) and Elvire by Marie Málková, Grossman's wife. With one exception (Jan Hrušínský's Pierrot, mentioned above) the characters all retained their original conception. With the departure of its leading stars Jiří Bartoška and Jana Preissová, the production lost some strongly marked individual performances but gained a more even-grained ensemble quality.

But it was not only the company that had changed. Between 1989 and 1992 Czechoslovakia had undergone the most sweeping political changes since the Second World War. So too, of course, had the theatre. While audience figures declined generally, the expectations that spectators brought to the theatre, and the significance they attached to it, were no longer the same. How could a production which had spoken to spectators whose daily lives were governed by the monotonous deceptions of a 'normalised' society still hold the same meaning for post-revolutionary audiences? It seemed to me that spectators in 1992 received the play in a more relaxed manner, but also that the performance elicited less laughter than formerly. This was evident, for example, in their reaction to Don Juan's speech about hypocrisy. Originally, the tirade was well understood by Czech audiences to be an analysis of the behaviour necessary for an individual to succeed in society, and as such had been greeted originally with laughter of recognition and derision. But this was no longer the case in 1992. By way of explanation, it would be better to let a Czech spectator speak:

> [In 1982] there was a subconscious need by spectators to laugh at the people who, without any tolerance, make decisions for other people. I am not one of those who laugh aloud; nevertheless, in this laughter I heard the need for a union which did not exist. It was also a demonstration of a basic and very useful weapon of the oppressed against the oppressor: derision. Everyone is afraid of it. But now the audience simply do not laugh as much as they did. On the other hand, we can feel the fear that these moral principles still prevail. If, some time ago, Don Juan's words could also have been interpreted as a kind of instruction on how to vegetate in a non-functioning society, now they are much more an attack on the conscience of everyone present, because everyone has a share in the former situation and – why not say so? – also guilt. Juan's monologue becomes a standard by which everyone measures their own guilt.[85]

Since the real purpose and ultimate justification of theatre is to provide a forum in which societies represent themselves, it is hardly suprising that what spectators saw in 1992 was the same production but with a subtly altered meaning. Grossman's *Don Juan* serves as a useful reminder that it is not directors alone, nor playwrights nor actors, who give a theatrical event its meaning; its significance is created in the encounter of artists with a public in a particular society at a particular moment.

CHAPTER 4

'DON JUAN' AT LARGE ON THE TWENTIETH-CENTURY STAGE

Meyerhold's 1910 production is a landmark for theatre historians, but another celebrated Russian *Don Juan*, still remembered with immense affection by those who watched it, was Anatoli Efros' much-revived production at the Malaya Bronnaya Theatre in the 1970s. Efros was considered the purest of Russian directors, the one who spoke most directly to the Russian soul. His *Don Juan* was a subtle, multi-layered piece of theatre combining a rich psychological and emotional texture with indirect political comment. From Bulgakov's *A Cabal of Hypocrites* (1929) to Lyubimov's politically radical production of *Tartuffe* (1968), Russian theatre developed a sustained tradition of using Molière to raise political questions in an oblique way. Efros implied that the Statue could symbolise the authorities that Don Juan defies and, by implication, the dangers that confront artists who dare to defy official ideology. (Efros himself was expelled from the Lenin Komsomol Theatre for 'ideological deficiencies' in 1967). At another level he treated the story more as a timeless parable or morality tale. His Don Juan was an exhausted, atrophied soul, a former idealist no doubt, but not a militant rationalist. According to Efros, 'Don Juan dies because he devours himself, so to speak. He can no longer live because he has nothing to live for... He's losing his mind from not being able to find something to believe in.'[1] The Commander was not a miraculous moving Statue, merely an ordinary man dressed in plain clothes who enters Don Juan's house and takes him by the hand. Don Juan seemed intuitively to recognise in this prosaic figure the invitation to death that he had been waiting for. The main axis of the production, as often with Efros, was the contrasting personalities of the leading actors. Against Nikolai Volkov's hard, questing Don Juan, Lev Durov as Sganarelle was the eternal Oblomov, more open-hearted, gentle, unaggressive. This tragic *Don Juan* may have been an indictment of the betrayal of high ideals such as justice and humanity; or it could just as readily have been seen as a confrontation between two psychological types, the active and the passive.

In Czechoslovakia, *Don Juan* was long overshadowed by *Don Giovanni.* Ever since Mozart directed its première at the Estates' Theatre in Prague in 1787, the opera has held a special place in the city's cultural life. Nevertheless, a surprisingly rich performance tradition attests to an enduring Czech fascination with Molière's play. In 1790, probably as a result of interest aroused by Mozart's opera, it was the first of Molière's works to be performed in Czech.[2] The earliest Czech productions of *Don Juan* were given at a time when the play was still virtually ignored in France. It was performed in 1864 and 1890 at the Prozatímíní Theatre (Prague) and at the Na Veveří Theatre (Brno) in 1898, with further productions there in 1929 and 1937. J. Škoda also directed a long-running production in Brno during the Second World War. In Prague it was again staged in 1915 at the National Theatre, and at the Municipal Theatre in 1917 and 1940. In recent decades it has proved the most popular of all his plays with some thirty productions in Bohemia and Moravia since 1945, compared with twenty-five for the opera. The explanation may be that centuries of oppression and a long anti-clerical tradition find natural resonances in a play which, more than any of Molière's comedies, lends itself to criticism of authority and the ruling class.

Two productions of *Don Juan* stand out from the pre-war and post-war periods. One was an expressionist production by Karel Hugo Hilar at the Prague Municipal Theatre (Vinohrady) in 1917. The leading Czech director of the period, Hilar worked in partnership with the brilliant designer Vlastilav Hofman to create a stage based on painting and architectural techniques. Inspired by his interest in expressionist drama, Hilar based his interpretation on a tormented conflict between individual passion and the forces of moral order. The other major production, and one whose influence is still felt, was directed by Jaromír Pleskot at the National Theatre in 1957. In the title role was Otomar Krejča, of whom it was said: 'Krejča's Don Juan is revolt incarnate. In his solitary superiority, this Don Juan is not interested in the objects of his passion. He poses the question of man's freedom.'[3] But this was not about freedom in a purely metaphysical sense. Coming a year after the Twentieth Congress of the Communist Party in the USSR, when the crimes of the Stalinist period were for the first time partially admitted, Pleskot's interpretation boldly highlighted the abuse of power and the problem of individual responsibility. After the nine-year freeze following the Communist putsch of 1948 (a period of imposed Socialist Realism in the theatre), this production marked the start of a loosening of ideological control in the theatre which was to last until 1968.

In Slovakia, where it was first produced in 1942 (Slovak Popular Theatre, Nitra), *Don Juan* has appealed to a number of directors for whom re-workings of the classics offered one of the few permitted avenues for the expression of political non-conformity. A long-running production by the Slovak National Theatre (Bratislava, 1972) emphasised the degeneracy of Don Juan as the representative of a decadent ruling class. While the National Theatre's version followed Molière's text faithfully, recent Slovak productions have adopted a more radical approach in eliminating the miraculous and resolving Don Juan's fate by human means: in one, an uprising of villagers who impersonate the Commander to kill the anti-hero; in another, a deception by Don Juan himself who feigns death in order to re-appear under a new guise later; or yet another where Don Juan was knocked down and killed by a car when crossing a busy street. All these versions testify to an abiding desire to make the play a direct comment on contemporary social reality.

In this respect perhaps the most penetrating analysis was made in

Don Juan 87 directed by Vladimír Strnisko at the Štúdio Novej Scený (Bratislava, 1987). At the centre of this interpretation was a critique of European rationalism, of which *Don Juan* is an early dramatic embodiment – or rather, an indictment of the way the rationalist tradition had become debased by the Communist regime to the level of calculating pragmatism. In Strnisko's eyes, Don Juan's manipulative intellect epitomised the self-serving corruption which the regime had legitimised. Don Juan was seen not as an exceptional, epic character but as a paradigm for something that permeated through every level of society:

> For me, Don Juan was a model character through whom it was possible to represent the world of big and small Don Juans, all aspiring – naturally – to the best social system in the history of mankind ... whereas, in fact, all their fine words are nothing but a shop-front for the most colossal fraud in the history of humanity, a system for deriving personal benefits with impunity... If someone had to kick us out of work, he never told us directly; instead he would wrap it up in an ideological construct... The spectators suddenly recognised Don Juan in those who serve the system, in their professors, directors, secretaries. Through Don Juan people saw their 'masters' in a new perspective. They were daily tormented by the same lies and driven to the subordinate status of servants who had to believe, or at least pretend to believe.[4]

Strnisko, too, eliminated the *deus ex machina*. Don Juan escaped punishment and resumed his selfish way of life protected by his mask of hypocrisy which, as the text says, 'is how a sensible man makes the most of the vices of his time'. The Statue's role as an embodiment of old-fashioned authority was vested in an ineffectual Don Louis, while Don Juan's real moral adversary was Sganarelle. It was he who opposed the former's pragmatism by defending the lost spiritual values of mankind. One of the key characters in this interpretation was the Beggar, whom Strnisko saw as a symbol of those who stay faithful to their principles despite intense pressure to make them bend. But in an ironic twist, the Beggar appeared as a steely-grey corpse making it an ambiguous symbol, to say the least. The director explained: 'The corpse is a symbol of faith which sets the direction without having any concept of compass points. It sets the direction but keeps changing it; so, with the direction changing, all we are left with is blind faith.'[5]

This was ten years after the founding of Charter 77 (a fact alluded to in the title of *Don Juan 87*) and two years before the 'Velvet Revolution' which ended the Communist party rule.

In German-speaking countries Benno Besson has continued to direct some of the most exciting *Don Juans.* After staging his own adaptation in Rostock and with the Berliner Ensemble, Besson later returned to Molière's original play, in a new translation by himself and Heiner Müller. This text was used in Besson's productions at the Deutsches Theater in 1968 and the Vienna Burgtheater in 1986. For the Berlin production Besson took the idea of Don Juan as a comic figure, which was already a central element in the first Brecht–Besson version, and sharply accentuated the ridicule and the overall sense of fun. It was a much freer, less didactic, and more transparently theatricalist staging, with scenes played downstage under powerful spotlights, and using frontal delivery and improvised playing to break the barrier between stage and auditorium. The new production style led to some dilution of the rigorous historical analysis of the fable, especially since Besson was now using Molière's more ambiguous text rather than his own adaptation where the social issues were exposed explicitly. Conversely, it offered a richer and more complex theatrical experience. The anti-hero, played by Reimar Baur, was still a narcissistic seducer radiating splendour and cocooned in self-love. So immense was his ego that whenever he spoke he turned his face to the audience to bask in their adulation. Besson equipped him with a mirror dangling over his penis which enabled him to reflect light from the centre of his being on to the faces of female spectators who caught his attention. These inventive touches typify Besson's theatrical method of taking an idea, developing it to its extreme, and embodying it in a concrete image or gesture. In the same vein, Pierrot's impotent frustration while Don Juan was seducing Charlotte was expressed by the peasant mutilating the cardboard trees of the scenery. Nor did Besson content himself with giving Don Juan an aristocratic costume but dressed him a whole succession of absurdly exaggerated high-fashion outfits and wigs. In contrast Sganarelle (Rolf Ludwig) was an unshaven, bedraggled wretch in an outfit of threadbare mud-coloured hessian. For the ending, Besson and his designer Gunter Kaiser staged an impressive show with noise, smoke and flickering flames. But for the atheist Don Juan, hell had lost all its terror and Reimar Baur showed a sublime contempt for the theatrical artifices that tried to engulf him. Prodding the devils with his sword, he made *them* shriek in pain. As he followed the Statue down the steps to hell, he paused to look around at the new world that beckoned and uttered an expansive 'Ah!' at the pleasures that he seemed to see awaiting him.

This, wrote the critic in *Süddeutsches Zeitung*, was Marxism with wit and a sense of fun.[6] Critics in East Berlin papers found it harder to accept Besson's departure from a strict socialist line. One compared it with the Berliner Ensemble production, and concluded that 'this version lacks rationalised transparency. It is less precise in its expression of critical intention, though richer in its theatricality.'[7] Another said sternly: 'By showing only socially negative behaviour, an opportunity is lost to develop the profitable lesson.'[8] 'It was a radiating, sparkling comedy', wrote a third, 'but this exquisite staging is too obtrusive; instead of being a vehicle for the fable it becomes a vehicle for the artist to display his skills.'[9]

In Besson's most recent *Don Juan*, his fifth production of the play and the first in his native French (Comédie de Genève and the Maison des Arts, Créteil, 1987), these tendencies were pushed to even greater extremes, turning the play into a grotesque pantomime-farce. It had a stunning performance from Philippe Avron who played Don Juan as an ageing travesty role. To begin with he gave a

Plate 19 Philippe Avron as Don Juan and Carlo Brandt as Sganarelle in Benno Besson's 1987 production (Geneva/Créteil).

preposterous caricature of an effete powdered marquis with a blond wig, falsetto voice and a brilliant repertoire of facial tics (plate 19). At first spectators saw only a decadent poodle but gradually the portrait grew in complexity and power. Avron revealed depths of cruelty in his handling of the peasants, and breath-taking insolence in the way he examined his make-up and touched up his lipstick while Elvire delivered her first-act recriminations. His thin voice gradually became firmer so the tirade against hypocrisy came across not so much as a petulant outburst but a fiery denunciation which had the force of an implacable character behind it. Apart from the latter, Besson turned everyone and everything to derision. Sganarelle (Carlo Brandt) was a tall, hunched figure who moved and talked like an idiotic giant; Elvire, a thigh-slapping Amazon determined to get Don Juan back into her bed in the first act, became a shrill hysteric in the fourth act; Don Louis was a decrepit, dribbling centuagenarian; and the Statue, tottering on high platform soles and inviting Don Juan to supper in a plummy tenor voice, brought the house down. Several critics felt that by going all-out for outrageous comic effect, Besson sacrificed the critical message. It is true that it was an exhilaratingly crude comedy – and as such far preferable to the cool academicism and unruffled elegance of Francis Huster's production which was playing in Paris at the same time. But it was also more than that: in its grotesquely distorted caricature of society and the derision it unleashed, it approached the ferocity of a Hogarth cartoon.

In Anglo-Saxon countries (Scotland apart), Molière has seldom fared well and *Don Juan*, with rare exceptions, even less well than better-known comedies like *Tartuffe*. David Phethean's 1972 production at the Bristol Theatre Royal used a new translation by Christopher Hampton first heard on BBC's Radio 3 in January the same year. The slightly surreal staging with costumes of mixed periods, a night club boasting *folies-bergères* dancers and music ranging from classical to jazz, enlivened the performance without contributing much to the audience's understanding. Four years later Robert Cordier directed the play in Hampstead. Jokey and entertaining rather than challenging, its main strength was Tom Conti's amiable, urbane Don Juan. Both these productions reflected a British awkwardness with Molière, an uncertainty which resolved itself in a characteristic tendency to facetiousness. More successful than either of these, because more morally ambiguous, was the National Theatre's production in 1981. In Alison Chitty's elegantly simple set (an empty wooden stage with overhead screens to display mood-setting projections), and under Peter Gill's gimmick-free directing, it allowed spectators to concentrate on the characters and the ideas. Gill accentuated the dramatic contrasts in the play by switching between high comedy of manners in the scenes with Don Juan and low comedy in the person of Ron Pember's clownish Sganarelle (a process facilitated by John Fowles' colloquial translation). By presenting Don Juan as a smooth-talking, courtly gentleman, the production confronted head-on the moral problems posed by the unstoppable egoist. London spectators also had a rewarding experience when the Georgian Film Actors' Theatre of Tbilisi brought their experimental *Don Juan* to the Almeida in 1989. In common with many productions in the former Soviet Union, it was less interested in the psychological or moral themes than the class issues. Don Juan was killed by Elvire's brothers at the Commander's tomb. The walking Statue, a prompter informed the audience, was just a story invented by the ruling class to keep gullible peasants in line.

The most impressive British production of *Don Juan* to date was directed by Ian McDiarmid at the Royal Exchange Theatre in Manchester (1988). Julian McGowan's visually superb setting was part-mausoleum with black marble columns suspended above the floor, and part-volcano with sulphurous fumes filtering up from gratings in the floor. In this apocalyptic setting, Jonathan Kent played a cold, sneering, ruthless predator. Bernard Bresslaw's Sganarelle, not a comic simpleton but a dignified and well-spoken humanitarian capable of searing irony, was at least the equal of his master. Bresslaw's performance was evoked thus: 'He is a hypnotic presence, radiating genial ineptness and childlike naivety, dwarfing his master in height and bulk, manoeuvring about the stage like an elephant on tiptoes.'[10] McDiarmid was interested in exploring the nature and implications of Don Juan's quest, which he rightly saw as a moral and intellectual one, and said:

> The most interesting and perhaps theatrical way of asking the question 'What is it to be moral?' is to place an immoralist on the centre of your stage and have arguments and moralists fall down before him. Not in order that the audience might approve of this but that they may ask themselves various questions about where the social critic ends and the fascist begins.[11]

With its Nietszchean undercurrents and superb theatricality, the play came across as a dark, disturbing masterpiece.

It is in France, inevitably, that the most sustained performance tradition has grown up. After the 'unlocking' of *Don Juan* by Jouvet and Vilar, the 1960s and 1970s saw a steady stream of productions, sometimes four or five in a single season, and spanning the entire spectrum of styles. Inevitably many of them were of only passing interest, such as Pierre Dux's horribly commercial boulevard production (Théâtre de l'Oeuvre, 1963) or the numerous honourable but routine productions. What follows is a small selection of some of the more successful or unusual variations on the theme.

Maurice Sarrazin, for example, took *Don Juan* as the basis for an intriguing experimental psychodrama on the theme of the social history of madness (Théâtre Daniel-Sorano, Toulouse, 1972). His treatment was inspired by Michel Foucault's *The History of Madness in the Classical Age* which documented the growing practice in Molière's time whereby a wide category of allegedly 'prodigal', 'unnatural', 'dissipated' or 'debauched' individuals were committed to institutions for the criminally insane. This mechanism of social cleansing provided the director with his angle of attack to approach the play: 'It was not through the man or the myth that I found the reality of the character, but through the society of the time and the systems it set in place for protecting itself from free-thinkers.'[12] Sarrazin adroitly carved the text up and re-constructed it as a psychiatric investigation conducted by the director of the Bicêtre mental prison at the request of Don Louis who wishes to have his reprobate son interned. The action began with the reading of an authentic contemporary indictment, but in which the name of Don Juan was substituted for the original. Then the other characters appeared before the tribunal to present their evidence by re-enacting the various episodes of Don Juan's debauch. A terrified Sganarelle, concerned only with saving his own skin, read out the Commander's condemnation. Sarrazin's experiment, showing interesting parallels with the Brook–Weiss *Marat-Sade*, offers an extreme illustration of the then current trend for directors to exploit existing texts freely as the basis of self-authored spectacles.

Of the many *Don Juans* from the Brechtian school, one of the most rigorous, apart from Chéreau's, was Bernard Sobel's at the Théâtre de Gennevilliers in 1973. Sobel was a Marxist director who had gone to the Berliner Ensemble in the 1950s to learn about theatre from Brecht. Like Brecht, he saw Don Juan as neither a militant atheist nor an enlightened pioneer of free thought, but rather a pernicious force who in himself is a mediocre person without merit or interest. He described him as 'a fop, the last of a race, not a revolutionary, hardly even a man in revolt. He clings to his privileges and abuses them. If he doesn't respect the code of behaviour of his class it's because he senses vaguely that feudal values, *gloire*, honour or virtue can only be empty facades for the domesticated aristocracy after the Fronde.'[13] Unlike Chéreau's Don Juan he was not a man in conflict with his own class nor, with his irredeemable banality, could he be seen as the critical conscience of his class. His function, like that of Brecht's anti-hero, was to betray unconsciously the decadence of his class.

The originality of Sobel's approach lay in its exploration of the relationship between the play's theatrical form and its ideological meaning. Sobel was particularly interested in the play's dramaturgical 'aberrations', i.e. its lack of classical unity and its unorthodox mixture of genres and styles. He argued that, far from being the product of faulty craftsmanship, these irregular features were devices employed by Molière to produce a 'de-centering effect' (to use Louis Althusser's terminology), whereby the image of contemporary society was decomposed into a series of critical reflections:

> The play's oddities start to become productive when one sees how the transitions from farce to seriousness, or from burlesque to tragedy, distance the spectators from what they see on stage and invite them not to experience feelings of 'fear' or 'pity' for the characters, in other words, not to believe in the illusion.[14]

In effect, Sobel was arguing that it was an early example of Brechtian alienation techniques.

Sobel therefore sought in the performance to exaggerate the discontinuity of dramatic styles and genres. Each scene was treated as a stereotypical specimen of its own genre – tragedy, morality play, vendetta play, pastoral or farce – thus exposing the artificiality of the dramatic conventions on which the play draws. The characters were not treated as psychological entities but as role-types (the valet, the father-figure, the avenger, etc.) reduced to *commedia dell'arte* essences. The entire performance, in fact, became a complex representation of theatre-within-theatre. Actions were played in a second degree of reality, the actors 'quoted' their roles demonstratively, and scenic convention was exposed as such:

> Painted cardboard rocks part to reveal statues silhouetted against a skycloth, the wronged virgin wrings her hands, a noble father beats his breast in the candlelight, the peasants speak their dialect the way the Court loves to hear it.[15]

By these means, said Sobel, the production 'reveals starkly what theatre is: a place where you can see an ideology taking shape in the interplay of codes, mirrors and conventions'.[16]

Plate 20 A scene from Bernard Sobel's production (Gennevilliers 1973).

The production was recognised as a masterpiece of staging (plate 20). According to Guy Dumur: 'In its genre, it has a beauty and an accuracy that have never been surpassed.'[17] Critics were unanimous in praising the beauty of the costumes and lighting, and the reconstructed seventeenth-century stage on which it was performed. (Dumur affirmed that the set merited a place in the Musée des Arts Décoratifs). Its defect was that the company's dramaturgical analysis, for all its conceptual rigour, was translated into a performance that appeared mechanical and premeditated. What it lacked, perhaps, was the compelling overall vision and broader historical sweep of Chéreau's production to lift it above the demonstration of a theorem. It remains, nevertheless, one of the few stagings of its kind to bear comparison with Chéreau's.

A refreshingly different approach to the play was provided by Philippe Caubère, a member of the Théâtre du Soleil (Cartoucherie de Vincennes, 1977). In a sense it was a return to tradition, but a special form of theatrical tradition of the kind lovingly nurtured by the Théâtre du Soleil. As with the company's famous *1789* which recounted the French revolution through the eyes of strolling players, the story of Don Juan was performed as it might have been enacted by a troupe of players for a popular audience in the seventeenth century. Four actors and two actresses made up the entire cast. It was staged in a reconstruction of the interior of Molière's Palais-Royal theatre. Built originally for Ariane Mnouchkine's celebratory film about the playwright, *Molière, A Life*, this was not the stylised, deconstructed theatricalism of Sobel or Chéreau but a real wooden theatre smelling of candles and greasepaint. In front of the painted flats, the company of clowns put on period costumes, masks and false noses to enact the old story of Don Juan like a picaresque cloak and dagger adventure. This was an unashamedly entertaining *Don Juan* with a strong vein of farce as Molière probably intended. Caubère himself played Don Juan and gave a memorable caricature of a petit-marquis. Behind the white face mask lay nothing but the hollow shell of a dissolute parasite, so wasted and ravaged that he tottered precariously on his high heels and had to be supported by the other characters. Opposite him was the heavy bulk of Maxime Lombard's Sganarelle, a red-nosed *commedia dell'arte* buffoon with a Marseilles accent.

One expects the Théâtre du Soleil's work to be marked by outstanding performance skills, since it is the most disciplined and polished company of actors in France. This is not necessarily an unmixed blessing. The prodigious aesthetic perfection of Mnouchkine's more recent productions has diminished their popular appeal, making them dazzling but remote. What was remarkable about *Don Juan* performed as a farce was that it gave the play the vigour and directness of a popular entertainment without sapping its critical force. As Gilles Sandier noted: 'It's the farce itself that constitutes an iconoclastic denunciation of the myths of the age, and turns the religious and sexual morality of the time to derision.'[18] One of the most pleasurable of recent versions, it was hailed as 'truly popular, not intellectualised but highly intelligent'.[19] And, performed at Christmas time, it played to audiences of delighted children.

France's two leading directors of the last quarter-century, Antoine Vitez and Roger Planchon, have each presented versions of *Don Juan* in their own distinctive style. In both cases the play was a component of a wider programme of experiment with the classics. Vitez's numerous productions of Molière during the 1970s led him eventually to conceive the idea of a 'Molière cycle' which would be a summation and synthesis of his work. This exciting project, like all great discoveries, was based on an essentially very simple idea: that Molière's entire *œuvre* is created out of a number of elements that are re-composed over and over from one play to the next. From this, he said, came 'the idea of creating an ensemble in which one would recognise the different figures that make up Molière's universe, and also the moral, philosophical themes, and the theme-characters'.[20]

The sequence of four major plays (*School for Wives, Tartuffe, The Misanthrope* and *Don Juan*) was performed at the Avignon Festival in 1979 and then, in the autumn, at the Porte Saint-Martin theatre in Paris. Vitez did not want 'to do *my* Don Juan or *my* Misanthrope' but to stage the tetralogy as if it were a single work, with the same cast of twelve actors in a single setting. For the Paris production Claude Lemaire's design was an open stage with minimal props, backed by a painted *trompe-l'œil* classical edifice. The main interest of this experiment was the way it illuminated the unity of themes and situations in Molière's plays. Stripped to its essentials, Molière's drama is based on very elementary, ancient scenarios of farce, as old as Plautus and Terence: the jealous husband and the lover; the con-man and his victim, and so on. These primitive theatrical schemas are also the key to the archetypal situations and human characters of Molière's world and to its thematic unity, woven from certain recurrent moral issues (religion, sexuality, money, power) which re-appear at different points in the tapestry. Thus, Don Juan's hypocrisy echoes Tartuffe's, and his desire to dominate other people echoes, in an aristocratic register, the tyrannical impulses of Arnolphe the bourgeois guardian in *School for Wives*.

It would be impossible to summarise Vitez's interpretation of *Don Juan*, since it had no independent significance outside the web of inter-textual references that made up the whole cycle. A flavour of his thinking is given by his journal entry where he notes: 'Don Juan and Alceste. They are both consumed by the same flame. Martyrs, both of them. Their speeches are similar.'[21] Or speaking of *Tartuffe* and *Don Juan*:

> *Tartuffe* could be played after *Don Juan*, inverting the order of composition. After playing Don Juan the same actor would reappear as Tartuffe and it would be Don Juan, after his speech in praise of hypocrisy in the fifth act, after escaping from Hell, who returns to earth wearing the mask of a *dévot*; and indeed it *is* him.[22]

Thus, Don Juan combined aspects of Alceste in his defiance of society, and of Tartuffe in his defiance of God. Molière's heroes, as conceived by Vitez, all have something of the holy fool in them. Their folly is an impossible passion which, in a Quixotic way, they attempt to live out in an uncomprehending world. 'It's always the story of Knights errant', Vitez wrote.[23] Theatrically, this common motif translates into a situation which is the same in each play, and which Vitez defines as the enactment of a definitive moment in the life – in effect, the death, literal or metaphorical – of its martyred hero:

> Each play is the story of a single day. It recounts *the day when*. There is no before, no afterwards. For instance *The Misanthrope* is the day when Alceste is seen for the last time in the world. As if each play recounts someone's death.[24]

This was really the work of a theatrologist investigating how a series of masterpieces worked. Vitez described himself as 'more a metaphysician than a sociologist' and saw his productions as being in the tradition of Jouvet rather than Planchon. In many respects his work with Molière bore this out. It shunned both spectacular staging concepts and *a priori* ideological readings. In their place it offered a functional setting and an open exploration of the text by the actors in performance. Without setting out to prove anything with *Don Juan*, Vitez created a production of intense theatricality in which the tragic interpretation of Molière's work was counterbalanced by the exhilaration of the actors' encounter with the text.

With Roger Planchon's long-awaited *Don Juan* (1980) one returns to the mainstream mode of critical *mise en scène*. But even theatre-goers familiar with the director's style were astonished by its conceptual and scenic richness, and the sheer monumental grandeur of its staging. Planchon presented *Don Juan* alongside Racine's *Athalie* in a diptych representing contrasting treatments of the theme of religion and power. As with Vitez's Molière cycle, the interest lay in the juxtaposition of the component works. Ostensibly the two plays, one Catholic propagandist and triumphalist, the other straining at the very limits of belief, could not be more dissimilar. In fact, if one accepts the Marxist premise that history, rather than the Romantic notion of individual creative inspiration, is the primary shaping force behind art, they are the opposite sides of the same coin. It could hardly be otherwise since, Planchon says:

> All creative artists in a given age have the same material at their disposal, the same elements like building blocks. Each of them builds in his own manner and in the end their houses are both different and yet similar.[25]

His idea in bringing the plays together was to explore how a shared ideological context was mediated differently by their respective authors. In fact, the two plays are not quite contemporaneous. *Athalie* (1690) represents the triumphant phase of the forces that scored an early victory with the suppression of *Don Juan* (1665). It 'explains' *Don Juan* by offering a vivid evocation of the spiritual totalitarianism that called forth dissenters like Don Juan. (With typical historical precision, Planchon specified that Don Juan was a blasphemer not an atheist. He could be seen as a fore-runner of eighteenth-century atheists, but the idea of a mid-seventeenth-century atheist is an anachronism). Reciprocally, *Don Juan* 'explains' *Athalie* by presenting an archetypal manifestation of the stirrings of dissent that militant Catholicism mobilised itself to suppress.

The plays were performed on alternate nights with the same cast. The setting for both was a remarkable *décor à machines* designed by Ezio Frigerio. Its centrepiece was a giant gold-painted cupola modelled on St Peter's in Rome, resting on black marble friezes. Under this all-embracing symbol of the Counter-Reformation was another permanent element over which a skeleton kept watch: a black marble tomb waiting to receive the two blasphemers, Athalie and Don Juan, at the end of each performance. Within this monumental setting, Planchon staged a succession of scenes of great plastic beauty. When the action switched from interior to exterior, the cupola was raised and the walls parted to reveal the different scenes: in *Don Juan*, a forest, a sea-scape with giant waves frozen as if about to crash down and engulf Don Juan, a palace or simply the sky. Christian imagery of a heavily baroque character abounded everywhere – a crucified Christ watching over Don Juan's temptation of the beggar, a death's head that was revealed when the Commander's tomb opened, a scene laid out like Leonardo's *Last Supper* when the Commander came for supper with Don Juan. The action was interrupted periodically by solemn liturgical and funeral processions to the accompaniment of organ music. The eloquent stage picture with which *Athalie* ended was of an angel dressed in golden armour, holding a giant cross, standing atop a canon. It was by such images of triumphant Catholicism in *Athalie* that Planchon shed light on Don Juan's struggle, a few years earlier, against the gathering forces of spiritual totalitarianism.

With its monumental operatic quality, this production marked a summit of baroque scenic richness. But Planchon has generally been more successful than many directors (Sobel, for instance) in maintaining a balance between outer spectacle and inner human reality, between the ideological concept and the core of individual experience. This is important because, for theatre to achieve any profound resonance in the spectator, it is not enough to dismantle the mechanisms of an ideology. In addition (and here the comparison with Sobel is illuminating) it must convey a sense of the way ideological forces are experienced by people in their lives. If Planchon achieved this in *Don Juan*, it was thanks to the remarkable performances of Gérard Desarthe (Don Juan) and Philippe Avron (Sganarelle). Avron set out a very believable Sganarelle who was neither grotesque nor stupid, but a man with an uncomplicated acceptance of the tenets of his faith – the epitome, as Planchon said, of 'the ordinary man whose faith is nothing other than the common sense of his age, in other words the dominant ideology of his time'.[26] As Don Juan, Gérard Desarthe gave a moving interpretation of a courageous man facing his own extermination. This was not Vilar's affirmation of the atheist's freedom but the death agony of an individual condemned by his fellow men, and whose only freedom is to utter defiant blasphemies. The moral, Planchon said, is this: 'It is clear that the play summons every atheist today to reflect on an age when a man did not defy God with impunity.'[27]

In contrast to Planchon, and at the extreme boundaries of theatre as a transcendent metaphysical experience, Maurice Bénichou, a member of Peter Brook's international company, directed a subtle and suggestive *Don Juan* at the Bouffes du Nord in 1984. Devoted to the theme of death, the production echoed Brook's concept of theatre as an actor-centred ritualistic enactment of the cosmic mysteries of man's existence. Bénichou's Don Juan was a man who insists on asking questions about the ultimate meaning of existence, and pays for it with his life. Visually, the production evoked the ambiance of Brook's mythic theatre in the creation of a performance area defined by natural materials such as sand, pebbles and a tree, and the use of cosmic symbols of water, fire and sky. The production made one experience the play in a new way largely thanks to the peculiar sense of inner calm and authority that Brook's actors convied, aided by their proximity to the audience in the Bouffes du

Nord's Greek-style arena. Presenting it as a timeless sacrificial ritual, Bénichou nearly succeeded, as very few directors have, in extracting the play from its social and historical context.

These productions illustrate the immense diversity of theatrical experiment which Molière's play has inspired. Even so, the catalogue is far from being exhaustive. Other experiments which could be mentioned include Arlette Téphany's all-female production with the Théâtre en Liberté (1975) or André Burton's playboy-style production evoking the fashionable 1960s resorts of St Tropez and Val d'Isère (Théâtre de l'Esprit Frappeur, Brussels, 1970). With electronic music and gadgetry, a Commander figure who appears on a television screen, and death that comes in the form of a road accident, it marked a tendency which is periodically in vogue to up-date classical texts in the most literal and superficial sense. Looking further afield, Richard Foreman mounted a deconstructionist *Don Juan* in the style of his Ontological–Hysteric Theatre (Guthrie Theatre, New York 1983). More recently, the Yaoundé International Theatre from Cameroon set the action in a modern-day African village with a white Cartesian Don Juan in an otherwise black African cast (Avignon Festival, 1992). In an explosive confrontation of ancient and modern, of European and African mythology in a racial and cultural stew, and its allusions to AIDS, the play became a striking metaphor for life in the late twentieth-century global village. At the time of writing the Comédie-Française is preparing a new staging for the 1990s. There is a familiar ring to the pronouncements of its director Jacques Lassalle: *Don Juan* is 'the most Shakespearean work of the French repertoire'[28] and 'the most modern of Molière's plays'.[29] Thus does Don Juan continue its apparently infinitely renewable stage life.

CONCLUSION

In the modern secular world, as Shaw realised at the start of the century, Don Juan is defunct as a mythic figure.[1] As we have seen, however, the frequent assertions of his death have not prevented Molière's play from being put to a multitude of new uses. Passionately re-discovered and re-invented, *Don Juan* has undergone a remarkable succession of mutations on the modern stage. The diversity of interpretation to which this study attests will be echoed in the impressions of any theatre-goer who has a sustained experience of the play in performance. As one production succeeds another, one hears the familiar words being spoken without ever having the sensation of seeing the same drama. The same is true, up to a point, of any play, yet I do not think it would be argued that *The Cherry Orchard* or *Endgame* (which all too often lead directors into the trap of a shorthand 'Chekhov style' or 'Beckett style') are susceptible to such radical re-definition. In part, the wide spectrum of interpretations which it engenders reflects the heteroclitic nature of Molière's play with its unusual concoction of philosophical speculation and social satire. It is this diversity of subject-matter and variety of objects of interest, rather than the mere ambiguity of the central character, that make *Don Juan* not just an elastic play but one whose core is capable of very substantial displacement according to the angle of view.

It is probably not by accident that the re-discovery of Molière's play and its continued popularity coincide with a period in which directors have been the dominant power in theatre. The features mentioned above make *Don Juan* a director's play *par excellence.* There are limits to the extent to which even the most submissive directors like to have their role prescribed and *Don Juan*, as well as posing considerable theatrical challenges, certainly offers directors immense interpretative freedom. Indeed, it is a text which not only invites directorial initiative but positively demands a strong directorial vision. In straightforward rendition the play all too readily appears amorphous, its dramatic focus uncertain and its ideas diffuse. Conversely, the most successful productions have usually been those where a director with a firm grasp has seized the text and bent it to a particular conception. There is undoubtedly a sense in which this is a minimising operation, and it can be objected that the play is diminished by it. Yet it seems to be a necessary condition of the process which, as Pirandello put it, 'releases the dramatic text from its irremediable fixity' and resurrects it in a living performance.

Experiments with the classics engender strong feelings, negative as well as positive. Since many of the productions discussed in this study have been controversial, and since directors in general have tended in recent years to be demonised for their autocratic powers, their role in the enterprise demands a few more words here. The tendency of some reviewers (especially in France, and especially in relation to the French classics) to consider the dramatic work as having a fixed essence and to evaluate performances in terms of their fidelity to a putative 'correct' reading, overlooks two glaring facts. The first is that intepretation can not be avoided. The act of staging a play necessarily involves selecting from a pool of meanings, all of which are available to the reader but not all of which can be rendered coherently in a single performance. The second, as Jan Kott argued thirty years ago in his influential study *Shakespeare, our Contemporary*, is that 'classical' works are not classical because they embody an unchanging universal truth but because they are perpetually being renewed. (*Hamlet* is often cited as the *locus classicus* of a play which, as Peter Hall said, 'turns a new face to each decade' and acts like 'a mirror which gives back the reflection of the age that is contemplating it'.[2]) In denying the need to re-interpret texts for one's own time, the essentialist notion of the classics as unalterable entities really amounts to condemning them to be exhibits in a cultural museum.

What, then, are the boundaries of legitimate creative experiment? Are there any limits to the range of admissible readings? On a theoretical level none at all. As soon as it is conceded that there is not one correct reading but a multiplicity of legitimate interpretations, the possibilities become theoretically infinite. In practice, interpretations which work against the text rarely exceed the status of limited experiments – legitimate, since all experimentation in art is legitimate, and interesting for other reasons, but of marginal significance in terms of their capacity to illuminate the play. The greatest productions, those which have captured the assent of audiences and defined the play for them, can be seen in retrospect to have worked with the text and against tradition. In other words, they have taken an unfamiliar perspective on the text through which spectators' recognition of their own world fuses with their recognition of the world of the play.

As for the play discussed in this book, its changing faces are so varied as to make them well-nigh impossible to categorise. In a very schematic way, it is possible to discern three interpretative models. One involves productions where metaphysical and moral issues are at the fore, and which offer a humanist approach to the subject-matter. The productions of Jouvet, Bourseiller, Bergman and Grossman, in their different ways, have all been centred on the existential experience of the central character. Watching Don Juan grappling with the meaning (or, more often, non-meaning) of his destiny, the spectator is invited to reflect on the purpose and finality of human existence. A second model can be distinguished in productions where the primary emphasis shifts from the individual to the collective and the social. Rather than the ontological perspective of the first group, they adopt a historical or ideological approach to the subject-matter. Implicitly with Meyerhold, and explicitly with

Brecht, Besson, Chéreau and Sobel, what gives the story its interest is the light it sheds on the society of the time and the contribution this makes to spectators' understanding of their own society. A third production-type is one where the theatricalist motive predominates. Meyerhold's attempts to formulate a modernist theatrical aesthetic with *Don Juan* have a counterpart in Vitez's deconstructionist exploration of the text and Bergman's and Caubère's celebration of theatrical tradition. In an age when the nature of theatrical discourse itself has become a major preoccupation of directors, the unorthodox dramatic form of *Don Juan* (like another re-discovered baroque play of the period, Corneille's *Comic Illusion*) gives the play a special appeal.

Obviously, no individual production is ever as one-dimensional as this schematic outline implies. Meyerhold's *Don Juan* was the expression of an experimental aesthetic *and* a critical reflection on tsarist society through the prism of the play. Vilar's exploration of the central character's atheism, although not framed in explicit ideological terms, was driven by a social purpose. In fact, good theatre will always appeal on several levels in which the social and political, the transcendental and the theatrical are somewhere involved. It is the balance between these that is constantly being re-formulated. In this sense, the production history of *Don Juan*, beyond the different performance aesthetics of its individual directors, offers a paradigm for the continuing attempt to define the place and function of theatre in society.

APPENDIX: GEOGRAPHICAL–CHRONOLOGICAL LIST OF PRODUCTIONS

This is a selective list, for reasons of space. In addition to those discussed above, I include details of some of the more significant or unusual productions.

AUSTRIA

27 July 1983, Landestheater, Salzburg. Director: Ingmar Bergman. Design: Gunilla Palmstierna-Weiss. Music: Rudolf G. Knalb. Michel Degen (Don Juan), Hilmar Thate (Sganarelle), Birgit Doll (Elvire), Erwin Faber (Gusman), Erich Hallhuber (Don Carlos), Klaus Guth (Don Alonse), Franz Kutschera (Don Louis), Gundi Ellert (Charlotte), Olivia Grigolli (Mathurine), Gerd Anthoff (Pierrot).
Transferred to Residentztheater, Munich, in autumn. See pp. 132–6.

18 June 1986, Burgtheater, Vienna. Director: Benno Besson. Trans.: B. Besson and Heiner Müller. Design: Ezio Toffolutti. Music: José Berghmans. Karlheinz Hackl (Don Juan), Kurt Sowinetz (Sganarelle), Brigitta Furgler (Elvire), Oliver Stern (Gusman/Don Carlos), Detlev Eckstein (Don Alonso), Horst Christian Beckmann (Don Louis), Barbara Crobath (Charlotte), Regina Fritsch (Mathurine), Caroline Koczan (Pierrot), Robert Meyer (M. Dimanche).

FORMER CZECHOSLOVAKIA

1917, Vinohrady Municipal Theatre, Prague. Director: Karel Hilar. V. Vydra (Don Juan), B. Zakopal (Sganarelle).

3 July 1958, Národní Divadlo, Prague. Director: Jaromír Pleskot. Design: F. Tröster. Otomar Krejča (Don Juan).

1982, Hradec Kralové. Director: Jan Grossman. Oldrich Vlach (Don Juan), Jan Novotný (Sganarelle).

1987, Štúdio Novej Scený, Bratislava. Director: Vladimír Strnisko. Milan Lasica (Don Juan), Marián Labuda (Sganarelle).
See pp. 157–9.

1989, Na zábradlí, Prague. Director: Jan Grossman. Design: Ivo Žídek. Costumes: Irena Greifová. Music: Carl Orff. Jiří Bartoška (Don Juan), Ondřej Pavelka (Sganarelle), Jana Preissová (Elvire), Zdeněk Dušek (Gusman), Jan Přeučil (Carlos), Vladimír Dlouhý (Alonso), Vlastimil Bedrna (Don Louis), Zuzana Bydžovská (Klara), Tereza Brodská (Markéta), Pavel Zedníček (Filip), Oldřich Vlach (Nedela), František Husák (Beggar).
Revived with cast changes 1992. See pp. 138–54.

FRANCE

15 Feb. 1665, Palais-Royal. Probable cast: La Grange (Don Juan), Molière (Sganarelle), Du Parc (Elvire), Louis Béjart (Don Louis), Du Croisy (Don Alonse/Pierrot), Armande Béjart (Charlotte), Mlle de Brie (Mathurine), De Brie (La Ramée).
See pp. 7–12.

17 Nov. 1841, Odéon. Director: Robert Kemp. R. Kemp (Don Juan).
See p. 13.

15 Jan. 1847, Comédie-Française. Director: Régnier. Design: Ciceri. Edmond Geffroy (Don Juan), Samson (Sganarelle), Mme Volnys (Elvire).
Revived with cast changes 1853, 1858, 1868. See pp. 13–15.

15 Jan. 1917, Comédie-Française. Director: Raphaël Duflos. Design: Désiré Chaineux. R. Duflos (Don Juan), Georges Berr

(Sganarelle), Jeanne Delvair (Elvire).
Revived with cast changes 2.1.1922 and 13.5.1925. *See pp. 15–16.*

21 Dec. 1922, Odéon. Director: Firmin Gémier. Design: Walter-René Fuerst. Music: Mozart. Jean Debucourt (Don Juan), Raoul Marco (Sganarelle), Mlle Andreyor (Elvire), Mlle Nevarre (Charlotte), Mlle Vermell (Mathurine), Grouillet (Pierrot).

1941, Compagnie du Regain (touring in the occupied zone). Director: Christian Casadesus.

20 March 1944, Théâtre du Vieux-Colombier. Director: Jean Vilar. Design: J.-P. Audouit/Maurice Coussonneau. J. Vilar (Don Juan), Jean Daguerre (Sganarelle), Jandeline (Elvire).
See pp. 34–6.

24 Dec. 1947, Théâtre de l'Athénée. Director: Louis Jouvet. Design: Christian Bérard. Costumes: Irène Karinski. Music: Henri Sauguet. L. Jouvet (Don Juan), Fernand-René (Sganarelle), Andrée Clément (Elvire), Pierre Renoir (Don Louis), Yvette Etievant (Charlotte), Dominique Blanchart (Mathurine), Jacques Mauclair (Pierrot).
See pp. 18–32.

5 Nov. 1952, Comédie-Française. Director: Jean Meyer. Design: Suzanne Lalique. Jean Debucourt (Don Juan), Fernand Ledoux (Sganarelle), Maria Casarès (Elvire), J-P Jorris (Don Carlos) Jean Yonnel (Don Louis), Micheline Boudet (Charlotte), Nelly Vignon (Mathurine), Robert Hirsch (Pierrot).
See pp. 66–71.

15 July 1953, Festival d'Avignon. Director: Jean Vilar. Design: Camille Demangeat/Léon Gischia. Music: Maurice Jarre. J. Vilar (Don Juan), Daniel Sorano (Sganarelle), Monique Chaumette (Elvire), Georges Riquier (Gusman), Jean Deschamps (Don Carlos), Roger Mollien (Don Alonse), Georges Wilson (Don Louis), Zanie Campan (Charlotte), Christiane Minazzoli

(Mathurine), Michel Bouequet (Pierrot), Philippe Noiret, M. Coussonneau, André Schlesser, J.-P. Moulinot, J.-P. Darras. *See pp. 36–48.*

1964, Centre Dramatique du Nord. Director: André Reybaz. Set/costumes: Raymond Renard. A. Reybaz (Don Juan), Serge Martel (Sganarelle), Eva Reybaz (Elvire), J.-P. Girard (Gusman), Bruno Sermonne (Don Carlos), Jean Menaud (Don Alonse), Jean Cabanis (Don Louis), Brigitte Defrance (Charlotte), Arlette Renard (Mathurine), Christian Chevreuse (Pierrot).
After Vilar, the play became a frequent choice for directors committed to decentralised 'théâtre populaire'. Other successful provincial productions of the 1960s included those of Jean Deschamps (touring, 1960), Gabriel Monnet (Comédie de Bourges, 1962), Jean Dasté (Comédie de St-Etienne, 1964), Pierre Barrat (Comédie de l'Ouest, 1969).

24 Feb. 1965, Théâtre de la Culture de l'Ile-de-France (touring). Director: Robert Manuel. Design: François Ganeau. Georges Descrières (Don Juan), Fernand Raynaud (Sganarelle), Danielle Volle (Elvire).
A great popular success. Interesting pairing of Descrières, a sociétaire of the Comédie-Française, with music-hall artist Raynaud.

1965, ORTF. Tele-film. Director: Marcel Bluwal. Michel Piccoli (Don Juan), Claude Brasseur (Sganarelle), Annouk Ferjac (Elvire).
Legendary television production, popular on account of star casting and influential in its dark, sinister dramatisation. Mozart's Requiem set the tone. The cinematic adaptation, with episodic adventures linked by the motif of a journey on horseback, resembled a seventeenth-century road movie.

4 Feb. 1967, Comédie-Française. Director: Antoine Bourseiller. Design: Oskar Gustin. Georges Descrières (Don Juan), Jacques Charon (Sganarelle), Ludmila Mikael (Elvire), J.-P. Zehnacker (Gusman), Serge Maillat (Don Alonse) Ivan Varco (Don Carlos), Michel Etcheverry (Don Louis), Agathe Natanson

(Charlotte), Annette Pavy (Mathurine), J.-P. Roussillon (Pierrot), Michel Aumont (M. Dimanche), J.-L. Jemma, Louis Eymond, F. Cerdal, J.-N. Sissia, D. Betourne, Nicole Gay.
See pp. 71–80.

3 Jan. 1969, Théâtre du Huitième, Lyon, (co-production with Théâtre de Sartrouville). Director: Patrice Chéreau. Design: P. Chéreau/Richard Péduzzi. Costumes: Jacques Schmidt. Gérard Guillaumat (Don Juan), Marcel Maréchal (Sganarelle), Roséliane Goldstein (Elvire), Jacques David (Don Carlos), Alexis Nitzer (Don Alonse), Jacques Debary (Don Louis), Michèle Oppenot (Charlotte), Sylvie Fischer (Mathurine), Bernard Ballet (Pierrot); Georges Guéret (Gusman), Julien Verdier, Roland Legrain, Jacques Jourdan, André Marié, Jacky Insermini.
See pp. 51–65.

12 Nov. 1970, Théâtre du Midi. Director: Stellio Lorenzi. Design and costumes: Pace. Bernard Verlay (Don Juan), André Gille (Sganarelle), Monique Morisi (Elvire), Henri Nassiet (Don Louis), Myriam Boyer (Charlotte), Nadine Servan (Mathurine), Guy Saint-Jean (Pierrot).
An amiable Don Juan and engagingly droll Sganarelle, but a somewhat under-directed production with little sense of gravity.

23 Nov. 1972, Théâtre Daniel-Sorano, Toulouse. Adapted and directed by Maurice Sarrazin. Design: Yvon Aubinel. Louis Granville (Don Juan), Christian Marc (Sganarelle), Elsa Berger (Elvire), Jacqueline Benoit (Charlotte), Pierre Fleurot (Pierrot).
See pp. 164–5.

8 May 1973, Théâtre 13 (Paris). Director: Roger Mollien. R. Mollien (Don Juan), J.-C. Sachot (Sganarelle), Martine Noiret (Charlotte), Jacqueline Jouet (Mathurine), Dominique Economides (Pierrot).
Unusual combination of baroque staging and actor-centred production in commedia dell'arte *style, praised for its honesty and sincerity.*

1 July 1973, Festival des Nuits de Bourgogne (Dijon). Director: Michel Humbert. Robert Pagès (Don Juan), M. Humbert (Sganarelle).
Quasi-Artaudian sensory production presenting Don Juan as a victim of a repressive social mechanism.

9 Nov. 1973, Théâtre Municipal de Gennevilliers. Director: Bernard Sobel. Design: Bernard Thomassin. Costumes: Pierre Cadot. Didier Sandre (Don Juan), Christian Colin (Sganarelle), Hélène Vincent (Elvire), J.-P. Ancelle (Don Carlos), Jacques Emin (Gusman/Don Alonse), Yves Kerboul (Don Louis), Agathe Alexis (Charlotte), Stéphanie Loik (Mathurine), Alain Maratrat (Pierrot).
See pp. 165–7.

1975, Théâtre en Liberté. Director: Arlette Téphany. A. Téphany (Don Juan), Evelyne Istria (Sganarelle), Evelyne Grandjean (Charlotte), Noëlle Hussenot (Mathurine), Claude Cendras (Pierrot).
All-female cast. The director described her production as 'feminine but not feminist'.

23 Dec. 1977, Cartoucherie de Vincennes. Director: Philippe Caubère. Design: Guy-Claude François. P. Caubère (Don Juan), Maxime Lombard (Sganarelle), Clémence Massart (Elvire/Charlotte), Jonathan Sutton (Don Louis/Don Carlos), Françoise Jamet (Gusman/Mathurine/Don Alonse/Mme Dimanche), J.-C. Bourbault (Pierrot/Beggar/Statue).
See pp. 167–9.

17 July 1978, Festival d'Avignon. Director: Antoine Vitez. Design: Claude Lemaire. J.-C. Durand (Don Juan), Gilbert Vilhon (Sganarelle), Nada Strancar (Elvire), Daniel Martin (Don Carlos), Richard Fontana (Don Alonse), Marc Delsaert (Don Louis), Dominique Valadié (Charlotte), Jany Gastaldi (Mathurine), Daniel Soulier (Pierrot).
Théâtre de la Porte Saint-Martin (Paris), Sept.-Dec. 1979. See pp. 169–71.

26 May 1979, Comédie-Française. Director: J.-L. Boutté. Design: J.-L. Boutté/Philippe Kerbrat. Music: Dominique Probst. Francis Huster (Don Juan), Patrice Kerbrat (Sganarelle), Catherine Ferran (Elvire), Philippe Etesse (Don Carlos), Joël Demarty (Don Alonse), Jacques Toja (Don Louis), Christine Murillo (Charlotte), Catherine Salviat (Mathurine), Gérard Giroudon (Pierrot), Raymond Acquaviva, Dominique Rozan, Yves Gasc, Laurent Lévy.
See pp. 80–91.

29 April 1980, TNP (Villeurbanne). Director: Roger Planchon. Design: Ezio Frigerio. Gérard Desarthe (Don Juan), Philippe Avron (Sganarelle), Brigitte Fossey (Elvire), Cathy Boset (Charlotte), Dominique Messali (Mathurine).
See pp. 171–3.

16 May 1984, Bouffes du Nord. Director: Maurice Bénichou. Design: J.-G. Lecat. Costumes: Françoise Tournafond. Music: Marius Constant. Niels Arestrup (Don Juan), Claude Evrard (Sganarelle), Irina Brook (Elvire), M. Bénichou (Pierrot), Luc Delhumeau (M. Dimanche), Pierre Dios (Gusman), Joséphine Fresson (Mathurine), H. Girardot (Don Carlos), J.-P. Klein (Don Alonse), Geneviève Mnich (Charlotte), Robert Murzeau (Don Louis), Thierry Murzeau, Georges Trillat.
See pp. 173–4.

10 Sept. 1987, Bouffes du Nord. Director: J.-L. Moreau. Francis Lalanne (Don Juan), J.-L. Moreau (Sganarelle), Anne Le Guernec (Elvire), Arnaud Giovaninnetti (Don Carlos), Francis Dermon (Don Alonse), Bernard Fresson (Don Louis), Fabienne Tricottet Charlotte), Sophie Renoir (Mathurine), Nicolas Vaude (Pierrot).
A riotous production, notable for pop star Francis Lalanne's interpretation of an androgynous Don Juan.

3 Oct. 1987, Maison des Arts, Créteil. Director: Benno Besson.
First performed in May at the Comédie de Genève (q.v.).

6 Oct. 1987, Théâtre Renaud-Barrault. Director: Francis Huster. Design: Hervé Boutard. Music: Dominique Probst. Jacques Weber (Don Juan), Francis Huster (Sganarelle), Fanny Ardent/Elizabeth Rodriguez (Elvire).
A reverential treatment of a classic, staged in homage to Jouvet. One critic said 'it's Don Juan *at the waxworks'.*

9 May 1988, Théâtre National de Marseille. Director: Marcel Maréchal. Design: Nicolas Sire. Costumes: Patrice Chaucetier. Pierre Arditi (Don Juan), M. Maréchal (Sganarelle), Aurelle Doazan (Elvire), Hubert Gignoux (Don Louis).
Revived 27.9.88 (Théâtre MC 93, Bobigny). A warm, actor-centred, life-affirming production. Superb performances from Maréchal and Arditi. Maréchal said: 'I want to bring out the indissoluble bond between Don Juan and Sganarelle. They fuse together like a couple, like childhood friends, they share the same need to listen to the other, talk to the other, learn from each other.'

1990, Théâtre Daniel-Sorano, Toulouse. Director: Jacques Rosner. Design: Max Schoendorff. Gérard Desarthe (Don Juan), Michel Boujenah (Sganarelle).
Transferred to Théâtre National de Chaillot, 10.1.91. Rosner intended to 'recapture the original scandal, the sacrilegious power that it had in 1665' (programme). Despite Desarthe's presence and Boujenah's clownish Sganarelle, the production was deemed a major disappointment. 'No originality, no point of view'; 'a classical matinée performance'; 'it lacks soul'.

9 Oct. 1993, Comédie-Française. Director: Jacques Lassalle. Design: Rudy Sabounghi. Andrzej Seweryn (Don Juan), Roland Bertin (Sganarelle), Jeanne Balibar (Elvire), Jean Dautremay (Gusman/Francisque/M. Dimanche), Thierry Hancisse (Don Carlos), Olivier Dautrey/Franck Manzoni (Don Alonse), François Chaumette (Don Louis/Statue), Catherine Sauval (Charlotte), Isabelle Gardien (Mathurine), Gérard Giroudon (Pierrot)
Première 9.7.93, Avignon Festival.

GERMANY

15 May 1952, Volkstheater, Rostock. Adapted and directed by Benno Besson. Design: Heiner Hill. Joseph Noerden (Don Juan), Norbert Christian (Sganarelle), Isolde Günter (Elvire), Martin Ernst (Gusman), Heinz Behrens (Don Alonso), Lothar Bellag (Don Carlos), Siegfried Göhler (Don Louis), Erni Wilhelm (Charlotte), Ruth Bauer (Mathurine), Hans-Theo Timmermann (Pieter), Helga Reichardt (Angelika), Erich Gutte (Dimanche), Werner Röwekamp (Marphurius), Erika Dunkelmann (Serafine).
See pp. 111–12.

19 March 1954, Berliner Ensemble. Director: Benno Besson. Design: Heiner Hill. Erwin Geschonneck (Don Juan), Norbert Christian (Sganarelle), Sabine Thalbach (Elvire), Alfred Land (Gusman), Ekkehard Schall (Don Alonso), Lothar Bellag (Don Carlos), Geor Auguste Koch (Don Louis), Regine Lutz (Charlotte), Käthe Reichel (Mathurine), Heinz Schubert (Pieter), Barbara Berg (Angelika), Hans Hamacher (Dimanche), Wolf Kaiser (Marphurius), Carola Braunbock (Seraphine).
See pp. 112–24.

1957, Landesbühne, Niedersachsen-Sud. Director: Reinhold Rüdiger. Eberhard Schwab (Don Juan), Rolf Jülich (Sganarelle), Marianne Weber (Elvire).

1968, Deutsches Theater, Berlin. Director: Benno Besson. Design: Gunter Kaiser. Reimar Joh. Baur (Don Juan), Rolf Ludwig (Sganarelle), Jutta Hoffmann (Elvire), Jürgen Hentsch (Carlos), Reinhardt Michalke (Alonso), Gerhard Beinert (Don Louis), Gudrun Ritter (Charlotte), Volkmar Kleinert (Pierrot).
See pp. 159–60.

25 Sept. 1983, Residentztheater, Munich. Director: Ingmar Bergman.
For details see Austria, 27.7.83.

GREAT BRITAIN

2 Jan. 1972, BBC Radio 3. Trans.: Christopher Hampton.

1972, Theatre Royal, Bristol. Director: David Phethean. Trans.: Christopher Hampton. Design: Alex Day. Tom Baker (Don Juan), John Nettles (Sganarelle), Helen Christie (Elvire).

7 April 1981, National Theatre. Director: Peter Gill. Trans.: John Fowles. Design: Alison Chitty. Music: George Fenton. Nigel Terry (Don Juan), Ron Pember (Sganarelle), Di Trevis (Elvire), Leonard Fenton (Gusman/M. Dimanche), Patrick Drury (Don Carlos), Robert Swann (Don Alonso), Michael Gough (Don Louis), Elizabeth Estensen (Charlotte), Holly de Jong (Martha), David Troughton (Peter).
See p. 163.

14 April 1988, Royal Exchange Theatre Company, Manchester. Director: Ian McDiarmid. Trans.: John Fowles. Design: Julian McGowan. Music: Jeremy Sams. Jonathan Kent (Don Juan), Bernard Bresslaw (Sganarelle), Katherine O'Toole (Elvire), John Pickles (Gusman/M. Dimanche), John Elmes (Don Carlos/Peter), Mark Aiken (Don Alonso), Randal Herley (Don Louis), Michelle Fairley (Charlotte), Mary Brennan-Moore (Martha).
See pp. 163–4.

ITALY

Oct. 1970, Teatro Stabile, Trieste. Trans. and directed by Giulio Bosetti. G. Bosetti (Don Juan), Lino Savoranti (Sganarelle).
Bosetti's starting-point resembled Chéreau's: 'Don Juan is a progressive: he wants to destroy in order to build afresh ... society is opposed to men like him. It tries to eliminate them' (programme). Savoranti played a brilliant Sganarelle, 'like a rat trapped between his petit-bourgeois morality and awestruck fascination for his master' (Journal de Genève, 16.10.70).

RUSSIA

9 Nov. 1910, Alexandrinsky Theatre, St Petersburg. Director: Vsevolod Meyerhold. Design: Alexander Golovin. Music: Rameau. Yuri Yuriev (Don Juan), Konstantin Varlamov (Sganarelle), N. G. Kovalenskaya (Elvire), K. N. Vertychev (Don Carlos), M. A. Vldamirov (Don Alonso), L. N. Pavlov (Don Louis), E. I. Timé (Charlotte), V. A. Ratchovskaya (Mathurine), I. E. Ozarovsky (Pierrot), S. V. Bragin (M. Dimanche), V. A. Garlin (Beggar), K. N. Berliant.

Revived 1918 and 1932. See pp. 92–110.

1973, Malaya Bronnaya Theatre, Moscow. Director: Anatoli Efros. Design: D. L. Borovsky. Nikolai Volkov/Mikhael Kozakov (Don Juan), Lev Durov/L. Kanevski (Sganarelle), Vera Saltykovskaya/ O. Yakovlava (Elvire).

Numerous revivals during the 1970s and still in repertory in 1994. See pp. 155–6.

SWEDEN

4 Jan. 1955, Stadsteater, Malmö. Director: Ingmar Bergman. Design: Stig Nelson. Georg Årlin (Don Juan), Toivo Pawlo (Sganarelle), Berit Gustafsson (Elvire), Nils Nygren (Gusman), Oscar Ljung (Don Alonse), Bengt Schött (Don Carlos), Anders Frithiof (Don Louis), Harriet Andersson (Charlotte), Gunnel Lindblom (Mathurine), Åke Fridell (Pierrot).

See pp. 125–30.

24 Feb. 1958, Dramaten, Stockholm. Director: Alf Sjöberg. Jarl Kulle (Don Juan), Anders Henriksson (Sganarelle), Anita Bjork (Elvire).

24 Feb. 1965, China Theatre, Stockholm. Director: Ingmar Bergman. Design: Sven Erik Skawonius. Music: Daniel Bell. Georg Årlin (Don Juan), Ernst-Hugo Järegård (Sganarelle), Kristina Adolphson (Elvire), Einar Axelsson (Gusman), Sven Nilsson (Don Alonse), Hans Strååt (Don Carlos/Don Louis), Margaretha

Byström (Charlotte), Christina Frambäck (Mathurine), Axel Düberg (Pierrot).
See pp. 130–2.

SWITZERLAND

24 May 1978, Stadttheater, Basel. Director: Bernard Sobel. German translation by Benno Besson and Heiner Müller. Design: Bernard Thomassin. Norbert Schwientek (Don Juan), Hilmar Thate (Sganarelle), Verena Buss (Elvire).
Revival (in German) of Sobel's 1973 production at Gennevilliers. Thate (who acted Sganarelle in Bergman's 1983 production) played a nagging, aged mentor to his prodigal young charge.

5 May 1987, Comédie de Genève. Director: Benno Besson. Design: Ezio Toffolutti. Music: José Berghmans. Philippe Avron (Don Juan), Carlo Brandt (Sganarelle), Juliana Samarine (Elvire), Dominique Serreau (Gusman), Gilles Privat (Don Carlos/ M. Dimanche), Claude Vuillemin (Don Alonso/Le Pauvre), Alain Trétout (Don Louis), Sylviane Simonet (Charlotte/Ragotin), Françoise Courvoisier (Mathruine/La Violette), Emmanuelle Ramu (Pierrot/Spectre).
Co-production with the Maison des Arts, Créteil. See pp. 160–2.

NOTES

Note on translations: unless stated otherwise below, translations used in the text are my own.

'DON JUAN', 1665–1925

1. *The Last Days of Don Juan*, Nick Dear, director (Stratford, 1990).
2. Sieur de Rochemont (pseud.), *Observations sur une comédie de Molière intitulée le Festin de Pierre* (Paris: Pépingué, 18 April 1665).
3. Prince de Conti, *Traité de la comédie* (Paris: 1666).
4. The posthumous edition (1682) was heavily censored. The text of the first performance has been re-constructed using editions published in Amsterdam and Brussels.
5. *Le Coureur des Spectacles*, 8.1.1847.
6. *Paris-Théâtre*, 30.4.1874.
7. Letter to Gabriel Boissy, 12.1.22. Cit. M. Descotes, *Les Grands Rôles du théâtre de Molière* (Paris: Presses Universitaires de France, 1960), p. 72.
8. Gabriel Boissy, *Comoedia*, 4.1.17.
9. Ibid.
10. Ernest-Charles, *Opinion*, 20.1.17.
11. Jacques Copeau, *Registres II: Molière* (Paris: Gallimard, 1976), pp. 38–9.

MAJOR PRODUCTIONS ON THE MODERN FRENCH STAGE

1. Jouvet, *Témoignages sur le théâtre* (Paris: Flammarion, 1951), pp. 62–3.
2. *Introduction à la vie dévote*. The incident is related by R. Brasillach in *Animateurs de théâtre* (Paris: Correa, 1936), pp. 44–5.

3 Léo Lapara, *Dix ans avec Jouvet* (Paris: France-Empire, 1975), p. 204.
4 Text published in Charlotte Delbo, 'Mise en scène de *Don Juan* par Louis Jouvet', in R. Johnson, E. Neumann and G. Trail (eds.), *Molière and the Commonwealth of Letters* (University Press of Mississippi, 1975), pp. 575–82.
5 Paul-Louis Mignon, *Louis Jouvet, Qui êtes-vous?* (Lyon: La Manufacture, 1988), p. 144.
6 *Témoignages sur le théâtre*, pp. 34–5.
7 Brasillach, *Animateurs de théâtre*, p. 44.
8 'Notes sur *Don Juan*' (Collection Louis Jouvet, Bibliothèque de l'Arsenal).
9 *Témoignages sur le théâtre*, p. 32.
10 Mignon, *Louis Jouvet*, p. 161.
11 Thierry Maulnier, 'Le Don Juan de Molière et le nôtre', *Le Figaro Littéraire*, 21.2.48 (p. 2).
12 Jouvet, *Molière et la comédie classique* (Paris: Gallimard, 1965), p. 87.
13 Ibid., p. 93.
14 Brasillach, *Animateurs de théâtre*, p. 46.
15 *Molière et la comédie classique*, p. 85.
16 Ibid., p. 129.
17 Ibid., pp. 83–4.
18 Delbo, 'Mise en scène de *Don Juan*', p. 576.
19 Ibid.
20 Ibid., p. 577.
21 *Carrefour*, 24.12.47.
22 *Témoignages sur le théâtre*, p. 46.
23 B. Dort, 'L'œuvre de Vilar: une utopie nécessaire', *Cahiers Théâtre Louvain*, 56–7 (1986), p. 31.
24 Copeau, 'Le théâtre populaire', in *Registres* I (Paris: Gallimard, 1974), p. 285.
25 'Note de Service' dated 20.4.44. Reproduced in *Jean Vilar par lui-même* (Avignon: Maison Jean Vilar, 1991), p. 45.

26 Programme, Théâtre de la Bruyère, 1944. The notes were subsequently published in Vilar, *De la tradition théâtrale* (Paris: L'Arche, 1955), pp. 35–6.
27 Vilar to Claude Sarraute, *Le Monde*, 12.12.53.
28 Morvan Lebesque, *Carrefour*, 16.12.53.
29 Vilar, 'Réponses à un questionnaire sur le *Don Juan* de Molière', 1963, (unpublished).
30 Vilar to Jacqueline Michel, *Le Parisien Libéré*, 10.12.53.
31 Vilar to Jean Duvignaud, 'Molière et Shakespeare', *La Nouvelle NRF* (Oct. 1953), p. 714.
32 *Arts*, 17–23.12.53.
33 *Le Figaro Littéraire*, 19.12.53.
34 'Réponses à un questionnaire'.
35 *L'Avant-Scène*, 294 (Sept. 1963), p. 17.
36 *Jean Vilar par lui-même*, p. 145.
37 'Réponses à un questionnaire'.
38 Vilar, *Le Théâtre, service public* (Paris: Gallimard, 1975), p. 371.
39 Barthes, 'Le silence de Don Juan', *Les Lettres Nouvelles* (Feb. 1954), p. 265.
40 Ibid.
41 'Réponses à un questionnaire'.
42 Georges Lerminier, *Le Parisien Libéré*, 14.12.53.
43 *Le Parisien Libéré*, 21.7.53.
44 *Le Monde*, 21.7.53.
45 *Le Monde*, 14.12.53.
46 *Le Figaro Littéraire*, 19.12.53.
47 'Réponses à un questionnaire'.
48 Dort, 'Un théâtre majeur: le TNP à Avignon', *Les Temps Modernes* (Oct. 1953), p. 759.
49 'Note de service' dated 3.5.44 (unpublished).
50 *Le Parisien Libéré*, 21.7.53.
51 Max Favalelli, *Paris-Presse L'Intransigeant*, 15.12.53.
52 Morvan Lebesque, *Carrefour*, 16.12.53. The allusion is to Louis Jouvet's production.

53 'Entretien avec Roger Planchon', *Etudes* (Aug.–Sept. 1977), p. 220.
54 B. Brecht, 'L'achat de cuivre – entretiens à quatre sur une nouvelle manière de faire du théâtre, *Travaux*, 1 (1970), p. 111.
55 B. Dort, 'La mise en scène des classiques entre 1945 et 1960', *Revue d'Histoire Littéraire de la France*, 77.6 (1977), p. 1013.
56 Dort, *Théâtre Public* (Paris: Seuil, 1967), p. 33.
57 Interview with P. Chéreau, in P. Madral, *Le Théâtre hors les murs* (Paris: Seuil, 1969), p. 148.
58 Chéreau, 'Le théâtre de l'ambiguïté et de la mauvaise conscience', *Approches*, 10 (Jan.–Feb. 1969), p. 12.
59 Ibid.
60 Chéreau, in *Le Monde*, 5–6.1.69.
61 'Le théâtre de l'ambiguïté'.
62 Ibid.
63 Madral, *Le Théâtre hors les murs*, p. 149.
64 Chéreau, in *Le Figaro Littéraire*, 17–23.2.69 (p. 42).
65 *Le Monde*, 5–6.1.69.
66 B. Poirot-Delpech, *Le Monde*, 16.1.69.
67 Gilles Sandier, *L'Avant-Scène*, 593 (1 Sept. 1976), p. 38.
68 *L'Humanité*, 2.1.69.
69 *Le Monde*, 16.1.69.
70 'Le théâtre de l'ambiguïté'.
71 Marcel Maréchal, 'Comment j'ai joué Sganarelle', *L'Avant-Scène*, 593 (1 Sept. 1976), p. 73.
72 Ibid.
73 Ibid.
74 *Le Monde*, 5–6.1.69.
75 Programme.
76 Georges Joly, *L'Aurore*, 8.11.52.
77 Jean Gandrey-Rety, *Ce Soir*, 8.11.52.
78 *Le Monde*, 8.11.52.
79 Marcelle Capron, *Combat*, 8.11.52.
80 *Paris-Normandie*, 14.11.52.
81 *Samedi-Soir*, 13.11.52.

82 Ibid.
83 Jérôme Santeuil, *Arts*, 14.11.52.
84 *Le Monde*, 8.11.52.
85 Marcelle Capron, *Combat*, 8.11.52.
86 Guy Verdot, *Franc-Tireur*, 8.11.52.
87 Georges Joly, *L'Aurore*, 8.11.52.
88 *Le Monde*, 7.2.67.
89 Ibid.
90 *L'Aurore*, 28.1.67.
91 *Le Monde*, 7.2.67.
92 *France-Soir*, 31.1.67.
93 Jean-Jacques Gautier, *Le Figaro*, 7.2.67.
94 7.2.67.
95 *Le Nouvel Observateur*, 15–21.2.67.
96 *Le Monde*, 7.2.67.
97 Jacques Carat, *Preuves*, (April 1967), p. 47.
98 René Saurel, *Les Temps Modernes*, 250 (1967), p. 1708.
99 *Le Figaro Littéraire*, 19.12.67.
100 Dominique Nores, *Les Lettres Nouvelles*, (May–Nov., 1967), p. 174.
101 *Preuves*, (April 1967), p. 48.
102 Nores, *Les Lettres Nouvelles*, p. 174.
103 *Le Nouvel Observateur*, 15–21.2.67, p. 41.
104 Robert Abirached, *La Quinzaine Littéraire*, 23 (1 March 1967), p. 29.
105 Robert Kanters, *L'Express*, 13–19 Feb. 1967.
106 Nores, *Les Lettres Nouvelles*, pp. 172–3.
107 23.2.67.
108 *Carrefour*, 15.2.67.
109 *Le Nouvel Observateur*, 15–21.2.67, p. 41.
110 *Carrefour*, 15.2.67.
111 *Le Nouvel Observateur*, 15–21.2.67, p. 41.
112 J-L Barrault, *Souvenirs pour demain* (Paris: Seuil, 1972), p. 157.
113 Michel Cournot, *Le Monde*, 2.6.79.
114 François Chalais, *France Soir*, 4.6.79.

115 Gilles Sandier, *Le Matin de Paris*, 7.6.79.
116 Jean Vigneron, *La Croix*, 7.6.79.
117 Boutté to Marion Thebaud, *Le Figaro*, 15.5.79.
118 *France Soir*, 24.5.79.
119 Ibid.
120 *Le Figaro*, 15.5.79.
121 'Entretien avec José-Maria Flotats', *Comédie-Française*, 112 (1982), p. 18.
122 *The Financial Times*, 4.7.79.
123 Interview with Boutté, in *Don Juan*, ed. Christine Géray (Paris: Hatier, 1985), p. 96.
124 Ibid.
125 Ibid., p. 101.
126 Ibid.
127 Ibid, p. 104.
128 Ibid., p. 106.
129 Ibid.
130 *Le Figaro*, 15.5.79.
131 *The Financial Times*, 4.7.79.
132 'Entretien avec José-Maria Flotats', p. 17.
133 *Le Quotidien de Paris*, 12.7.82.
134 *Valeurs Actuelles*, 18.6.79, p. 48.
135 *France-Soir*, 8.7.82.
136 G[illes] S[andier], *Arts*, 7.6.79 (p. 6).
137 Ibid.
138 Guy Dumur, *Le Nouvel Observateur*, 11.6.79.

MAJOR PRODUCTIONS ON THE MODERN EUROPEAN STAGE

1 Valery Bebutov, in *Vstrechi s Meierkhol'dom* (Moscow: Iskusstvo, 1967), p. 79.
2 Quoted by M. Hoover in *Meyerhold* (University of Massachusetts Press, 1974), p. 56.
3 Meyerhold, *Perepiska 1896–1939* (Moscow: Iskusstvo, 1976), p. 29.

4 Meyerhold, *Stat'i, pis'ma, rechi, besedi*, 2 vols. (Moscow: Iskusstvo, 1968), I, p. 261.
5 18 November 1907 (Central State Archive for Literature and Art, cat. ref. TsGTM, no. 225640, 186).
6 'O priglashenii V. E. Meierkhol'da na imperatorskuiu stsenu', *Obozrenie teatrov*, 349 (4 March 1908).
7 *Peterburgskaya gazeta*, 24.4.1908.
8 *Meyerhold on Theatre*, trans. E. Braun (London: Methuen, 1969), p. 101.
9 Ibid., p. 99.
10 Ibid., pp. 51–2.
11 Ibid., p. 99.
12 Ibid.
13 Ibid., p. 104.
14 Rudnitsky, *Meyerhold the Director* (Ann Arbor: Ardis, 1981), p. 149.
15 *Meyerhold on Theatre*, p. 102.
16 Ibid., p. 104.
17 Alexander Golovin, 'Yuriev i *Don Zhuan*', in Yury Yuriev, *Yury M. Yuriev* (Leningrad: Priboi, 1927), p. 55.
18 *Meyerhold on Theatre*, p. 102.
19 Ibid., p. 102.
20 Ibid., p. 133.
21 Quoted by Yuriev, in Zapisky, 2 vols. (Leningrad-Moscow: 1962), II, p. 186.
22 *Zapisky*, II, p. 188.
23 Yury Belyaev, 'O chem Rasskazyval Gobelen', *Novoe Vremia*, 11.11.1910.
24 *Zapisky*, II, p. 187.
25 E. Timé, *Dorogi iskusstva* (Moscow-Leningrad: VTO, 1962), p. 164.
26 Golovin, 'Yuriev i *Don Zhuan*', p. 57.
27 Timé, *Dorogi iskusstva*, pp. 163–4.
28 *Zapisky*, II, p. 188.
29 This translation in Rudnitsky, *Meyerhold the Director*, p. 156.

30 L. Vasilevskii, 'Aleksandrinskii teatr: Don Zhuan', *Rech*, 11.11.1910.
31 A. Benois, 'Balet v Aleksandrinske', *Rech*, 19.11.1910.
32 Y. O. Malyutin, *Aktery moego pokoleniia* (Leningrad-Moscow: Iskusstvo, 1959), p. 84.
33 Benois, 'Balet v Aleksandrinske'.
34 S. Volkonski, 'Chelyovok na tsene', *Apollon* (1912), p. 72.
35 Rudnitsky, *Meyerhold the Director*, p. 155.
36 A. Kugel, quoted in Rudnitsky, *Meyerhold the Director*, p. 155.
37 Oliver Sayler, *The Russian Theatre* (London: Brentani's, 1922), p. 208.
38 Although the text is usually known as 'Brecht's *Don Juan*' (and was published in Brecht's complete works with Besson and Elizabeth Hauptmann named as collaborators) Besson has said that the adaptation was begun by himself 'entirely without Brecht's knowledge or assistance', and that it was later completed by him and Hauptmann with the help of Brecht (André Müller, (ed.), *Der Regisseur Benno Besson* (Berlin, 1975), p. 109). The Rostock programme gave Besson and Hauptmann as the names of the adaptors. But the text's genesis is complex and difficult to unravel fully. See, for example, J. Fuegi, 'Whodunit: "Brecht's" adaptation of *Don Juan*', *Comparative Literature Studies*, 11.2 (1974), pp. 159–72. As for the Rostock production, although it was a collaborative venture with the Berliner Ensemble, the staging was almost entirely the work of Besson. According to the latter: 'In the last days prior to the opening performance, Bertolt Brecht came with three assistants from the Berliner Ensemble and helped during the final rehearsals.' (Besson, *Jahre mit Brecht* (Willisau: Theaterkultur-Verlag, 1990), p. 85.)
39 B. Besson, *Jahre mit Brecht*, p. 84.
40 Ibid., p. 85.
41 Ibid., p. 109.
42 Brecht, 'Zu *Don Juan* von Molière', in *Gesammelte Werke* (Frankfurt: Suhrkamp, 1967), XVII, p. 1260.

43 Ibid., p. 1258.
44 For an analysis of the adaptation, see A. Subbioto, *Bertolt Brecht's Adaptations for the Berliner Ensemble* (London: MHRA, 1975).
45 Brecht, 'Zu *Don Juan* von Molière', p. 1257.
46 *Jahre mit Brecht*, p. 84.
47 Ibid., p. 118.
48 Brecht, 'Zu *Don Juan* von Molière', p. 1262.
49 Jürgen Rühle, *Der Morgen*, 23.4.54.
50 Ibid.
51 Hans Ulrich Eylau, *Berliner Zeitung*, 23.3.54.
52 I. Bergman, *The Magic Lantern*, trans. J. Tate (London: Hamish Hamilton, 1988), pp. 162–3.
53 *Helsingborgs Dagblad*, 2.2.73.
54 *The Empty Space* (London: MacGibbon & Kee, 1968), p. 65.
55 Per Erik Wahlund, *Svenska Dagbladet*, 5.1.55.
56 Interview, in L.-L. and F. Marker, *Ingmar Bergman. A Life in the Theatre* (Cambridge University Press, 1992), pp. 24–5.
57 Ebbe Linde, *Dagens Nyheter*, 5.1.55.
58 Ibid.
59 Herbert Steinthal, *Politiken*, 6.1.55.
60 M.N., *Arbetet*, 6.1.55.
61 *Dagens Nyheter*, 5.1.55.
62 Interview quoted in Henrik Sjögren, *Ingmar Bergman på teatern* (Stockholm: Almqvist & Wiksell, 1968), p. 294.
63 Ibid., p. 158.
64 Ibid.
65 *The Magic Lantern*, p. 241.
66 In Marker, *Ingmar Bergman*, p. 15.
67 'Das Spiel der Verlierer' (unsigned), programme, Residenztheater.
68 In Marker, *Ingmar Bergman*, p. 149.
69 In F. and L.-L. Marker, 'A long day's dying: Ingmar Bergman's *Don Juan*', *Theater*, 15.3 (1984), p. 40.
70 Ibid., p. 42.
71 Ibid.

72 In Marker, *Ingmar Bergman*, p. 154.
73 'Das Spiel der Verlierer'.
74 In Sjögren, *Ingmar Bergman på teatern*, p. 293.
75 In Marker, *Ingmar Bergman*, p. 19.
76 A statement made by Grossman's friend and associate Jindřich Černý, the director of the Czech National Theatre, in 'Jan Grossman', *Theatre Czech and Slovak*, 1 (1991), p. 11.
77 Evzen Turnovsky, 'Il teatro Na zábradlí', *Biblioteca Teatrale*, 22/23 (1991), p. 153.
78 Programme.
79 Personal communication, 19.9.92.
80 Martin Nezval, 'Poznámka k jedné inscenaci', *Právo Lidu*, 2.11.90.
81 Camus, *Le Mythe de Sisyphe* (Paris: Gallimard, 1943), p. 105. Quoted in programme.
82 Barbara Mazácová, 'Nanbevzet í Dona Juana', *Divadelní Noviny*, 1.2 (1992–3), pp. 1–11.
83 Aleš Kisil, 'Glosy k Donu Juanovi', *Svět a divadlo*, 2 (1990), p. 124.
84 Grossman, 'Kakfa's theatricality', *Divadlo*, 9 (1964), p. 8.
85 Martin Nezval, 'Poznámka k jedné inscenaci'.

'DON JUAN' AT LARGE ON THE TWENTIETH-CENTURY STAGE

1 Interview with Anatoli Efros, *Theatre Quarterly*, 7.26 (1977), p. 32.
2 Trans. Václav Thám, and performed in 1790 as a one-act play with ballet accompaniments.
3 Krauss, programme notes.
4 Vladimír Strnisko, 'Molière: Don Juan', in E. Šormová (ed.), *Don Juan and Faust in the XXth Century* (Prague: Czechoslovak Academy of Sciences, 1993), pp. 253–4.
5 Ibid., p. 254.
6 26.4.68.
7 Ernst Schumacher, *Berliner Zeitung*, 30.4.68.
8 Christoph Funke, *Der Morgen*, 25.4.68.
9 Rolf Dieter Eichler, *National Zeitung*, 30.4.68.
10 Grevel Lindop, *Times Literary Supplement*, 29.4.88.

11 Remarks made in 'In search of Don Juan', BBC 2, 7.1.89.
12 Quoted by M. Blain in *Analyses et réflexions sur le Dom Juan de Molière* (Paris: Editions Marketing, 1981), p. 202.
13 *Le Monde*, 9.11.73.
14 Ibid.
15 Jean-Pierre Leonardini, *L'Humanité*, 24.11.73.
16 *Le Monde*, 23.11.73.
17 *Le Nouvel Observateur*, 10.12.73.
18 *La Quinzaine Littéraire*, 272 (1 Feb. 1978), p. 19.
19 Ibid.
20 A. Vitez, 'Vitez on Molière', *Performing Arts Journal*, 13 (1980), pp. 81 and 84.
21 Vitez, 'Quatre fois Molière', *Europe*, 606 (1979), p. 177.
22 Ibid., p. 185.
23 Ibid.
24 Ibid., p. 176.
25 R. Planchon, 'Idéologie du pouvoir et pouvoir de l'idéologie', *Comédie-Française*, 92 (Oct. 1980), p. 30.
26 Planchon (interview with J-P Leonardini), *L'Humanité*, 18.11.80.
27 Ibid.
28 *L'Express*, 15.7.93.
29 *Comédie-Française*, Saison 1993–4.

CONCLUSION

1 G. B. Shaw, 'Epistle Dedicatory', *Man and Superman* (London: Constable, 1903).
2 *The Times*, 10.5.65.

SELECT BIBLIOGRAPHY

EDITIONS AND TRANSLATIONS CONSULTED

Molière, *Dom Juan*, in *Oeuvres de Molière*, ed. E. Despois and P. Mesnard, 13 vols. (Paris: Hachette, 1881-1912), V.

Molière, *Don Juan*, English trans. by Christopher Hampton (London: Faber, 1974).

Brecht, Bertolt, *Don Juan*, in *Gesammelte Werke*, ed. E. Hauptmann, 20 vols. (Frankfurt: Suhrkamp, 1967), VI. [In English, trans. R. Manheim: *Collected Plays*, ed. R. Manheim and J. Willett, in progress (New York: Pantheon, 1971), IX.]

SECONDARY CRITICISM

Arnavon, Jacques, *Le* Don Juan *de Molière* (Copenhagen: Gyldendal, 1947).

Bibliothèque Nationale, *Don Juan. Catalogue de l'exposition du 25 avril-5 juillet 1991*, (Paris, 1991).

Desportes, M. (ed.), *Analyses et réflexions sur* Dom Juan *de Molière* (Paris: Marketing, 1981).

Don Juan, Actes du Colloque de Treyvaux, 1981 (Editions Universitaires Fribourg, 1982).

Gnug, Hiltrud, *Don Juans theatralische Existenz* (Munich: Fink, 1974).

Horville, Robert, *Dom Juan de Molière, une dramaturgie de la rupture* (Paris: Larousse, 1972).

Mandel, Oscar (ed.), *The Theatre of Don Juan. A Collection of Plays and Views, 1630-1963* (Lincoln: University of Nebraska Press, 1986).

Obliques, 4, undated (1974?). Special 'Don Juan' issue.

Rousset, Jean, *Le Mythe de Don Juan* (Paris: Armand Colin, 1978).

Scherer, Jacques, *Sur le* Dom Juan *de Molière* (Paris: Société d'Edition d'Enseignement Supérieur, 1967).

Smeed, J. W., *Don Juan. Variations on a Theme* (London: Routledge, 1990).

Theatre en Europe, 19 (Feb. 1988). Special 'Don Juan' issue.

Villiers, André, Le Dom Juan *de Molière. Un problème de mise en scène* (Paris: 'Masques', 1947).

Weinstein, Leo, *The Metamorphoses of Don Juan* (Stanford University Press, 1959).

INDEX